A NIGHT OF HORROR

By Donald G. Rose

Copyright © 2016 Donald G. Rose
All rights reserved.
ISBN-10: 1533116423
ISBN-13: 978-1533116420

TABLE OF CONTENTS

Acknowledgements 5
Introduction 9
The Ohio Penitentiary 11
    Location and History 12
    Executions At The Prison 13
    Well Known Inmates 13
        General John Morgan 14
        William Porter 15
        James Snook 16
        Harry Pierpont, Charles Makley, And Russell Clark 17
        Bugs Moran 20
        Sam Sheppard 21
The Catastrophic Event 23
    The Fire 27
    Panic, Pain, Suffering and Death 43
    Help Given 47
    Shock And Anger 53
The Board of Inquiry 57
The Rebellion Following the Fire 77
The Continuing Investigation by The State Fire Marshal 131
    The Confession 137
The Trial 143
Epilogue 159
Blame 163
About The Author 165

Acknowledgements

Following are the main sources of information from which I learned the facts reported in this book:

The 727 page transcript of the proceedings of the Board of Inquiry appointed by Ohio's governor, Myers Cooper, which heard testimony for the five days immediately following the fire in an attempt to determine the cause of the fire and the reasons for the great loss of life.

The "REPORT ON THE OHIO STATE PENITENTIARY FIRE, COLUMBUS, OHIO, APRIL 21, 1930" prepared and published by the Ohio Inspection Bureau.

Articles published in the following Columbus newspapers concerning the fire and the events that followed:

- *The Columbus Evening Dispatch*
- *The Ohio State Journal*
- *The Columbus Citizen*
- *The Columbus Sunday Star*

The book entitled *Inside the Ohio Penitentiary*, written by David Meyers, Elise Meyers Walker, and James Dailey II, and published by The History Press.

The book entitled *Gold Medal Killer*, concerning the murder of Theora Hix committed by Ohio State University Professor James Snook. The book was written by Diana Britt Franklin and Nancy Pennell and was published by Marquette Books LLC.

Acknowledgements

I wish to thank the staffs of the Columbus Metropolitan Library and the Ohio History Connection for their help in directing me to their materials concerning the Ohio Penitentiary and the fire that is the subject of this book.

Several of the pictures in the book are from the collections of the Ohio History Connection. I wish to thank that organization for allowing me to use them and Lily Birkhimer for her help in getting me permission. Following is a list of those pictures and the designation of the particular collections in which they are found:

SC762:
Wagon stockade area
View of fire from Dennison Avenue (Front cover photo)
I&K Cellblock after fire
6th tier cell after fire
Firemen outside penitentiary
G&H Cellblock after fire
Prisoners observing victims
Attending to injured convicts
Fire victims in prison yard
Trucks taking bodies to fairgrounds
Corpses at the fairgrounds
Coffins at the fairgrounds
Convicts marching to breakfast
Tents burned by prisoners
Soldier outside administrative offices

SC 763:
Ohio Penitentiary postcard (Back cover photo)

SA 741 AV, Box 2, Folder 24B:

Acknowledgements

Ohio penitentiary

P339, Box 12:
Sam Sheppard photograph

Columbus Citizen microfilm collection:
Guard William Baldwin—April 22, 1930
Guard Thomas Little—April 22, 1930
Warden Preston Thomas—April 24, 1930
Women claiming bodies—April 25, 1930
National Guardsmen prepared for action—April 25, 1930
Naval reservists preparing for burial—April 26, 1930
Committee of Forty for Facts—April 28, 1930
Tents in stockade—May 1, 1930
Mike Dorn—May 3, 1930
Destroyed tents—May 8, 1930
Convicts Involved With Setting Fire—April 2, 1931
Hoskins with Grate, Gibbons and jailer—April 3, 1931
John Connors at Grate's trial—May 18, 1931
Drawing of Gibbons in solitary confinement—April 5, 1933

The following images appeared in the *Columbus Evening Dispatch,* or the *Ohio State Journal,* as indicated, and are used with the permission of *The Columbus Dispatch.* I want to thank the editor of the *Columbus Dispatch,* Alan Miller, for allowing me to use them, and I also want to thank Diana Hill, a member of the paper's staff, for her help in getting his permission.

The Columbus Evening Dispatch:
Amanda Thomas—November 9, 1926
Elizabeth Sampson—April 22, 1930
Prison ruins—April 22, 1930

Acknowledgements

Otto Gardner—April 23, 1930
Firemen on roof--April 29, 1930
Machine gun—April 29, 1930
Colonel Haubrich—April 29, 1930
Prisoners being transferred—April 30, 1930
Damaged cells—May 1, 1930
Franklin County Prosecutor, Donald Hoskins—May 8, 1930
Captain John Hall—May 28, 1930
Tacks Latimer—December 24, 1930
Prisoners returning to penitentiary—May 27, 1931

The Ohio State Journal:

Cellblock—April 22, 1930
Prisoners and cell doors—April 24, 1930
Deputy Warden Woodard—April 25, 1930
Penitentiary—April 27, 1930
Prisoners being transferred—April 27, 1930
Stockade--May 2, 1930
Warden Thomas and Colonel Haubrich—May 28, 1930

Several pictures are included through the Courtesy of "The Dailey Archives," the extensive collection of Ohio prison memorabilia, of which James Dailey II is the curator. I appreciate very much Mr. Dailey's willingness to allow me to use them. Each of the pictures included in the book from the archives is marked accordingly.

I am very thankful for the help and guidance I had from Doug McCready in formatting the book.

I also wish to thank my proofreaders: Mimi Mullin, Phyllis Hill, Linda Dayhuff, and Carol Scott for their excellent work.

Introduction

In writing a biography about my father, Judge Clayton Rose, Sr., I discovered that while he was an assistant prosecutor for Franklin County, Ohio, he was involved in the investigation of the cause of a fire at the Ohio Penitentiary in 1930 and was one of the prosecutors in the case that followed concerning the fire. In doing research for the book, I came to realize several things about the fire that led me to write this book:

1. It was a very significant event in the history of Ohio and the nation,
2. It is a very interesting story, and
3. Previous writings about the fire have concentrated on the tragedy of the fire itself and have given very little information about the rebellion that followed the fire, the state fire marshal's investigation into the origin of the fire, and the trial, which are essential elements of the story.

It is for those reasons that I have written this book.

I have reported the story from beginning to end. It is a complex story involving many people, and as in all such stories, the versions of the events given by witnesses vary somewhat. I have sifted through the various reports of the events that were involved in this tragedy and have endeavored to present the story as the events actually happened.

Donald G. Rose

The Ohio Penitentiary

Location and History

The Ohio Penitentiary, Columbus, Ohio
Courtesy of the Ohio History Connection

The Ohio Penitentiary was located in Columbus. It was built on a 22-acre site situated at the intersection of Spring Street and Dennison Avenue (now called Neil Avenue) only a few blocks from the intersection of Broad and High Streets, the main intersection in downtown Columbus and the location of the State Capitol. The penitentiary was completed in 1834 and served as a prison for 150 years.

The prison was originally designed for 1,500 prisoners, but usually had a far greater population. At the time of the fire, it housed 4,200 convicts. In the mid-nineteen fifties, the prisoner population reached its peak at a little over 5,200.

After ceasing to be used as a prison in 1984, it sat vacant for 14 years and was demolished in 1998.

Since 1998, significant development has taken place in the area where the penitentiary was located. It is now known as the Arena District of Columbus. Nationwide Arena, the home of the Columbus Blue Jackets, a National Hockey League team, is now located in that neighborhood. Also located within the area is Huntington Park, the home of the Columbus Clippers, a Triple A professional baseball team—a farm club for the Cleveland Indians. In addition, the neighborhood has various residential condominiums, office buildings, restaurants, and retail establishments.

Executions At The Prison

Prior to 1885 executions in Ohio were carried out by local law enforcement officials in the counties where the crimes took place and were done by hanging. An 1885 Ohio law specified that all future executions were to take place at the Ohio Penitentiary. Executions of both men and women began at the penitentiary at that time. From 1885 until 1897, executions at the penitentiary were by hanging. Beginning in 1897, condemned prisoners were electrocuted in the prison's electric chair known by prisoners and guards as "Old Sparky." A total of 28 hangings and 315 electrocutions took place at the penitentiary.

Well Known Inmates

During its 150-year history, the Ohio Penitentiary housed some well-known persons, including Confederate General John Morgan; William Porter, the writer of short stories known by his pen-name, O. Henry; Dr. James Snook; John Dillinger's gang members, Charles Makley, Harry Pierpont, and Russell Clark; "Bugs" Moran; and Dr. Sam Sheppard.

General John Morgan

During the American Civil War, Confederate General John Morgan organized and carried out raids for the purpose of attempting to divert Union troops who would otherwise be fighting at Vicksburg and Gettysburg. He and his raiders crossed the Ohio River into Union territory and carried out raids in Indiana and Ohio. His raids came to an end in Ohio. On July 19, 1863, the majority of his raiders were captured at Buffington Island, Ohio, when attempting to cross the Ohio River into West Virginia. The general avoided capture, but a week later, on July 26, he and his remaining raiders surrendered at Salineville, in Columbiana County, Ohio, about ten miles south of Lisbon.

General Morgan
Courtesy of the Dailey Archives

Morgan and his officers were taken to the Ohio Penitentiary and held there as prisoners of war. Morgan was imprisoned there until November 27, 1863, when he and six of his officers escaped from their cells by digging a tunnel under one of their cells to the prison yard and crawling through it. Once in the yard, they used ropes they had fashioned from bedding and an improvised grappling hook made from a fireplace poker to go over the penitentiary wall. Morgan and his officers then walked to nearby Union Station, bought train tickets, and went to Cincinnati, where Morgan re-crossed the Ohio River into Kentucky, his home state.

From there he continued south and eventually rejoined the confederate forces.

William Porter

William Porter, born September 11, 1862, was known for the many short stories written by him under his pen name, O. Henry. He was imprisoned at the Ohio Penitentiary from March 25, 1898 until July 24, 1901 for embezzling $1,150 from the First National Bank of Austin, Texas, while working there as a teller from 1891 to 1894. The embezzlement was established by an audit done after he had resigned his position with the bank. Porter was indicted, but he fled to New Orleans and from there to Honduras to avoid trial. He returned to Austin in February 1897 because his wife, Athol, who, because of her health had stayed in Texas when he fled, was then dying from tuberculosis, and he wanted to be with her. In Austin, he surrendered to the court. His father-in-law posted bail so he could stay by Athol's side. After his wife's death, Porter was tried and convicted. He was sentenced to five years in prison, and since it was a federal crime, the federal court determined where he would serve his sentence. The judge

O. Henry
Courtesy of the Dailey Archives

decided that he should serve it at the Ohio Penitentiary under an 1888 agreement with the State of Ohio for housing federal prisoners at the penitentiary. His sentence was reduced for good behavior, and he was released on July 24, 1901.

He had fourteen stories published under the name of O. Henry while at the penitentiary and continued to write under that name after his release. He sent his stories to a friend in New Orleans who forwarded them to publishers who had no idea the writer was in prison. It is not known for certain how he came up with the pen name, but it is widely believed that he constructed the name from OHio pENitentiaRY.

James Snook

James Snook was a 50-year-old professor of Veterinary Medicine at The Ohio State University. He was well-respected in his profession and was known for having invented the "Snook Hook," an instrument used in spaying animals that is still in use by veterinarians. He was also well known for having won two gold medals in the 1920 Olympics at Antwerp, Belgium, as a member of the United States pistol team.

Professor James Snook
Courtesy of The Ohio History Connection

A 24-year-old female medical student at the university, Theora Hix, did typing for him in order to earn money to help pay her school expenses. They became sexually involved. After a time, Snook, a married man, decided to end the relationship. Theora felt jilted and became difficult. One day, she tracked Snook down on the golf course at the prestigious Scioto Country Club. Snook's threesome, consisting of a prominent lawyer, a former state highway commissioner, and Snook were about to tee off from the fifth hole when a very angry Theora showed up and confronted Snook to his great embarrassment.

Snook apparently came to the conclusion that to be rid of her, the best thing for him to do was to kill her. Soon thereafter, on June 13, 1929, he took her to a secluded place and hit her several times on the head with a ball-peen hammer. Then, to make sure she was out of his life for good, he slit her throat.

He was indicted and tried for murder. John J. (Jack) Chester, the Franklin County Prosecutor, handled the prosecution. Because of the sensational nature of the case, it was extensively covered nationally by the newspapers. Snook was convicted and sentenced to death. He took his seat on "Old Sparky" on February 28, 1930.

Harry Pierpont, Charles Makley, And Russell Clark

Harry Pierpont, Charles Makley, and Russell Clark were members of John Dillinger's notorious gang. They participated with Dillinger in bank robberies and shoot-outs with the police.

In 1933, Dillinger was arrested in Allen County, Ohio, for robbery and taken to the county jail in Lima. Pierpont, Makley, and Clark broke him out of jail. During the break, Pierpont shot and killed the Allen County sheriff.

After the jailbreak, the Dillinger gang, including Pierpont, Makley and Clark went on a bank-robbing spree. In January 1934, in East Chicago, Indiana, during one of the robberies, a police officer was shot and killed. The gang fled to Arizona where they were arrested.

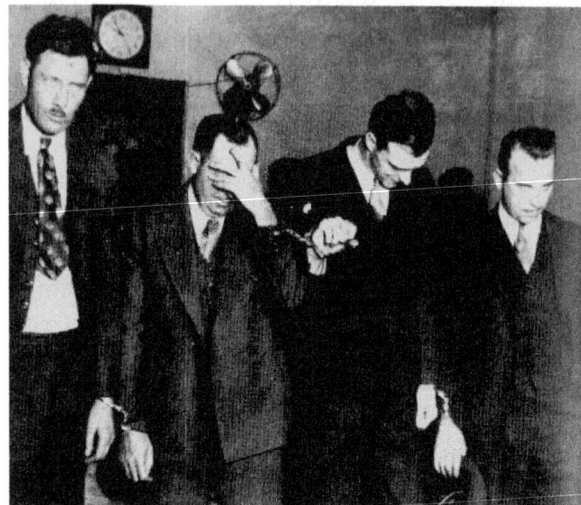

The Dillinger gang in a court room in Tucson, Arizona after their capture there -- Left to Right: Russell Clark, Charles Makley, Harry Pierpont, and John Dillinger
Courtesy of the Dailey Archives

Dillinger was taken to Indiana to stand trial for the murder of the police officer, but once again escaped from jail. Pierpont, Makley and Clark were returned to Ohio where they were tried for the murder of the Allen County sheriff and convicted. Clark was given a life sentence and was sent to the Ohio Penitentiary. Soon thereafter, Pierpont and Makley, who were sentenced to die in the electric chair, were also sent to the penitentiary.

Because it was feared that Dillinger would try to rescue his pals, Pierpont and Makley were transported to the penitentiary in a heavily armored 15-vehicle caravan, which included 50 armed National Guard soldiers. They arrived on March 27, 1934. Even after they were locked up in the penitentiary in Columbus, prison officials and the public feared that Dillinger, who had by then been proclaimed "Public Enemy Number One" and was considered sort of a miracle worker, would find a way to break them out. Additional security measures were taken at the prison.

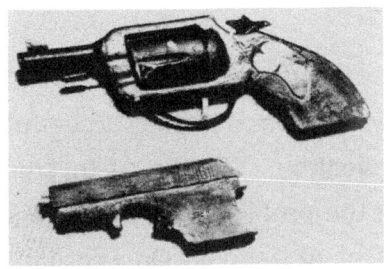

Fake weapons used by Pierpont and Makley
Courtesy of the Dailey Archives

Public rumors ran wild concerning plans supposedly being made by Dillinger to free them. On July 23, 1934, while Pierpont and Makley were awaiting their ride on the "humming bird" (another name for the electric chair), their leader, Dillinger, was shot to death outside a movie theater in Chicago.

In an attempt to avoid execution, Makley and Pierpont devised an escape plan. Copying a tactic used by Dillinger, they made fake guns and colored them with black shoe polish. They brandished the fake guns in their dash for freedom, which occurred on September 22, 1934, but were shot down by guards. Makley was killed. Pierpont was badly wounded, but lived to have his day sitting on "Old Sparky" on October 17, 1934.

Russell Clark when released from prison
Courtesy of the Dailey Archives

While they were preparing for their break, Pierpont and Makley invited

Clark to join them in their attempt. He declined, and they told him he was a fool. They said they were getting out of that "hell hole, one way or another," and he was going to have to spend 30 or 40 years there. Clark was released from prison 34 years later, on August 14, 1968.

Bugs Moran

Bugs Moran
Courtesy of the Dailey Archives

Bugs Moran was a highly successful and wealthy Chicago gangster during the prohibition era and was a rival of Al Capone. On February 14, 1929, in what has become known as the Saint Valentine's Day Massacre, seven members of Moran's gang were gunned down by members of Capone's gang. After the repeal of prohibition, Moran fell on hard times. On July 6, 1946, he was arrested for robbing the proprietor of the Silas Tavern located in Moraine, Ohio of $10,000. The tavern was across the road from a Frigidaire plant. The proprietor had gotten the $10,000 from a Dayton bank so that he could cash Frigidaire employees' paychecks. Moran and three others robbed him of the money. Moran was convicted and sent to the Ohio Penitentiary where he spent ten years as an inmate.

Sam Sheppard

Sam Sheppard, a doctor of osteopathic medicine at Bay View Hospital, in Bay Village, Ohio, a suburb of Cleveland, spent over ten years as a prisoner at the Ohio Penitentiary. He was found guilty of brutally murdering his pregnant wife, Marilyn, on the night of July 3, 1954 and was sentenced to life in prison for second-degree murder. The murder and trial drew nationwide attention from the media and the public. About ten years later, Attorney F. Lee Bailey filed a petition for a writ of habeas corpus in federal court and argued that the conviction should be set aside because Sheppard did not have a fair trial. The case was eventually decided by the U.S. Supreme Court, which found that the trial judge did not properly control his courtroom and that Sheppard's trial was conducted in a "carnival atmosphere" which deprived him of a fair trial, in violation of his right to due process.

Sam Sheppard
Courtesy of The Ohio History Connection

The Supreme Court set aside the conviction on June 6, 1966. Sheppard was subsequently retried and found not guilty. He was represented by F. Lee Bailey in the habeas corpus proceedings and at the retrial. Sheppard's story was the inspiration for the academy award winning movie, *The Fugitive*, and the television series of the same name.

The Catastrophic Event

The Catastrophic Event

The Ohio Penitentiary fire that occurred on Monday, April 21, 1930, killed 320 inmates. The fire ranks as the deadliest prison fire in the history of the United States and the third deadliest fire inside a building in United States history, behind only the Iroquois Theater fire in Chicago in 1903 that killed

The Ohio Penitentiary
Courtesy of the Ohio History Connection

602 and the fire at the Cocoanut Grove Night Club in 1942 that killed 492. There was a riot following the penitentiary fire, and during the riot, the governor turned control of the prison over to the National Guard. Sixteen days later, while the National Guard was in control of the prison, two convicts were shot to death while sleeping in their bunks when a National Guardsman accidentally fired a machine gun. That brought the death toll resulting from the fire to 322.

The fire was in New Hall, a brick building with stone trim, built in 1876 and located in the southwest portion of the penitentiary complex near the corner of Spring Street and Dennison Ave. It was 53 feet wide and 412 feet long and was parallel to Dennison Ave. (That portion of Dennison Ave. is now part of Neil Ave.) The building contained cellblocks G&H and I&K. Both cellblocks were free standing structures within the barn like building. They sat end to end, on a line parallel with Dennison Avenue. There was a ten-foot high wooden partition and a few feet of empty space separating the two cellblocks. Between the cellblocks and the walls of New Hall, there was about 10 feet of open space. Cellblock G&H was in the southern half of the building and Cellblock I&K was in the northern half.

The original cellblocks in New Hall had been removed and were being replaced with modern cellblocks with running water and toilets, which the original cellblocks didn't have.

The roof over the building was made of 1 ¼ inch tongue and grooved wood sheathing covered with slate. It was supported by 2-inch by 10-inch wooden trusses.

The new G&H Cellblock was completed seven months before the fire. The section designated "G" was parallel to the "H" section and was its mirror image. "G" was on the east side and "H" was on the

North side of G&H Cellblock before the fire
Courtesy of the Columbus Dispatch

The Catastrophic Event

west side. G&H Cellblock was 49 feet high and had six tiers. It was 176 feet long. The top of the cellblock was less than a foot below the wooden trusses supporting the roof. Each tier had a range of 17 cells on the "G" side and the same number on the "H" side for a total of 34 cells per tier. Hence, the six-tier cellblock had a total of 204 cells.

Each cell was eight-foot by eight-foot with an eight-foot ceiling. The cells were designed to house four convicts and had four folding bunks, four wooden folding chairs, a two-foot by two-foot wooden table, two shelves along the rear wall, a commode, and a washbasin. G&H Cellblock was designed for a maximum capacity of 816 men. When the fire began there were over 800 prisoners locked in G&H Cellblock, about 19% of the total population of 4,200 prisoners in the penitentiary at that time.

The six tier I&K Cellblock was under construction and unoccupied. Construction of that cellblock had progressed to the fifth tier. The construction-work was being done by men housed in G&H Cellblock.

As part of the construction project, the slate covered wooden roof over New Hall was to be replaced with a fireproof concrete slab roof. The heavier

Wagon Stockade Gate
Courtesy of the Ohio History Connection

concrete slab roof was to be constructed after the cellblocks were completed because the cellblocks were needed to help support the additional weight.

The Fire

On Monday, April 21, 1930, the day after Easter, in accordance with the usual routine, the horn signaling the end of the workday at the Ohio Penitentiary sounded at 4:00 p.m. The prisoners of G&H Cellblock prepared for dinner, went to the mess hall, ate dinner, and then returned to their cells and were locked in at about 5:00 p.m.

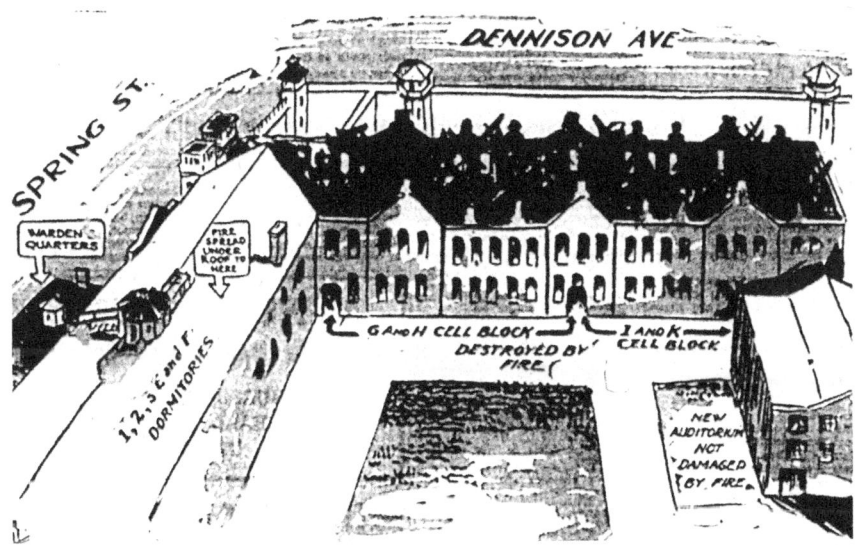

Location of Fire
Courtesy of the Columbus Dispatch

The fire started at the northwest corner of the partially completed and unoccupied I&K Cellblock at the top of the construction project, where flammable construction materials were located. Wooden forms used to shape concrete were stored in that area.

The Catastrophic Event

The forms had been treated with straw oil to make it easier to separate the concrete from the forms. The oil soaked forms, wood used for scaffolding, and eventually the roof constituted the fuel for the fire. The roof caught fire at the north end of I&K Cellblock, and the roof fire spread southward to Cellblock G&H.

The exact time when the fire was first observed is unknown. Estimated times varied between 5:20 p.m. and 5:40 p.m. Guard Hubert Richardson, stationed on the top of the G&H Cellblock, reported the fire to Thomas Watkinson, the day guard for G&H Cellblock who was on the ground level. Watkinson couldn't see any fire but ran toward the guardroom to report the fire. On the way he encountered Guard Augustus Light in E&F Dormitory, which lay between G&H Cellblock and the guardroom. At Watkinson's request Guard Light then reported the fire to the guardroom. Both Watkinson and Light estimated the time of reporting the fire to the guardroom as being a little after 5:30 p.m. When Watkinson turned back toward G&H Cellblock from E&F Dormitory, he was facing north and could then see a flame at the north end of I&K Cellblock, approximately 185 feet north of the north end of G&K Cellblock. He estimated the flame to be eight or nine inches high.

The first prisoner to notice the fire and notify the prisoners was Charles Shockey. He was on the second tier. He had the reputation of being a joker and wasn't taken seriously. Then Leo Lyons, a prisoner on the third tier immediately above Shockey stuck a mirror through the bars of his cell, saw the fire, and shouted, "HE'S RIGHT!" Later, prisoners noticed the reflection of the flames in the windows of a building across Dennison Avenue from the penitentiary.

Harold Whetstone, a guard in the tower atop the Spring Street wall, about midway along the wall, saw smoke coming from the I&K Cellblock. He estimated the time as being shortly after 5:30 p.m. He called the guardroom and reported it. A few minutes later, Whetstone again called the guardroom when he failed to hear fire trucks coming. Shortly afterward a guard in the prison yard fired his gun to alert people to the fire. Whetstone answered the gunshot by firing his gun and then called the guardroom for a third time because fire trucks were still not there.

The first fire alarm received by Columbus Fire Department was

The Ohio Penitentiary after the fire
Courtesy of the Columbus Dispatch

"pulled from a city box" located on Dennison Avenue, at its intersection with Dublin Avenue, at 5:39 p.m. A second alarm was

The Catastrophic Event

received by the fire department from within the penitentiary at 5:40 p.m.

[NOTE: Dublin Avenue is now part of Nationwide Boulevard.]

Fire equipment and firemen arrived within a couple of minutes after receiving the alarm and were admitted into the prison complex through the railroad stockade gate located at the north end of the prison. Equipment arriving after that entered through that gate or the wagon stockade gate at the corner of Spring Street and Dennison Avenue. The only other way into and out of the prison was at the entrance to the administrative offices on Spring Street, and that was only for pedestrians.

Fifty-eight-year-old Preston Thomas was the warden of the penitentiary at the time of the fire and had held that position for 17 years. His workday ended at 5:00 p.m. On the day of the fire, he left his office at 5:20 p.m. and went to his living quarters. He was there when, at 5:35 p.m., he was told of the fire. His living quarters were on the prison grounds in a building attached to the outside of the wall facing Spring Street, upstairs from the prison's administrative offices. He was on his porch, which faced Spring Street when he was told of the fire. He immediately went

Warden Preston Thomas
Courtesy of the Columbus Dispatch

to the guardroom, which was located in the same building. In the guardroom he was told that the fire was in I&K Cellblock. He stepped into the prison yard and observed the smoke. He asked if an alarm had been sent to the fire department and was told one had been sent. Then he ordered that a second alarm be sent and instructed guards, Thomas Little and William Baldwin, to take the keys for the cells in G&H Cellblock to the cellblock so the prisoners could be let out of their cells. He also ordered that the keys for the stockade gates be taken to the gates so fire equipment could be let in. The warden then went outside the walls to supervise efforts to prevent escapes. During and after the fire he directed efforts from outside and from the prison's administrative offices, but did not go inside the prison walls until Wednesday, two days after the fire.

For several weeks prior to the fire, the warden and other penitentiary officials had sensed that trouble was brewing at the prison. There had been several recent prison riots and attempted mass escapes around the nation, and they had received warnings that prisoners were plotting a mass escape from the Ohio Penitentiary.

The warden, in an effort to pacify the convicts, told the guards to create for the prisoners the best environment they could by being as friendly and obliging as possible. He increased the amount of food served to them and did what he could to improve its quality. He also increased the number of guards patrolling on the outside of the walls.

The warden also held conferences in the administrative offices at the penitentiary with representatives of the Columbus Police Department, the Columbus Fire Department, the Franklin County Sheriff's Office, the commander of the Regular Army troops at Fort Hayes (located in Columbus), officers of the National Guard,

The Catastrophic Event

and prison officials to discuss what to do in the event of an attempted prison break at the penitentiary.

Amanda Thomas, the warden's 34-year-old daughter, lived at the prison with her mother and father and performed various administrative tasks for her father. She also attended these meetings, and all agencies agreed they would accept a call from her if help was needed. As soon as she became aware of the fire, Amanda called police headquarters and Fort Hayes requesting assistance from the police and the military to help prevent a prison break. In response to her calls, police, Regular Army troops, and National Guard troops arrived at the prison in only a few minutes. The Columbus police quickly formed a cordon of 300 officers around the penitentiary, and military personnel stood by to assist as needed to prevent escapes.

Amanda Thomas
Courtesy of the Columbus Dispatch

Deputy Warden James Woodard
Courtesy of the Columbus Dispatch

It was approximately 5:45 p.m. when the warden went outside to supervise efforts to prevent escapes. Deputy Warden James

The Catastrophic Event

Woodard, second in command at the penitentiary, had gone to his mother's home in Kent, Ohio, for the Easter weekend and had not returned for duty but was due at 6:00 p.m. Sergeant Hostetter was next in command, followed by Sergeant Stroupe. They were at the prison, but their exact whereabouts were unknown. After the warden went outside, Amanda took charge of the matters at hand and gave orders until the arrival of the deputy warden. She went to the guardroom and issued weapons and ammunition, including sub-machine guns, to the guards and sent them to various posts. To discourage any attempt by the convicts to storm the gates, she sent several well-armed guards to each gate. She issued a shotgun to Tacks Latimer, a prisoner who served as a trusty, and posted him at the Spring Street entrance to the administrative offices.

When Deputy Warden Woodard arrived for duty at 6:00 p.m. he took charge. After Woodard's arrival, Amanda continued to provide what help she could. Among other things, she called the Columbus Physicians and Surgeons Bureau and asked them to spread the word to the doctors and hospitals in the Central Ohio area of the urgent need for medical services and supplies at the penitentiary. She was up all night and was still working at midnight on Tuesday.

Before the fire, Amanda had told friends that because of rumblings by the inmates, she and her dad and the other officials at the penitentiary, knew they were "sitting on a living volcano." After the fire she told them that when she heard the cry of fire and saw the yard filled with the most vicious black ugly smoke she had ever seen, she knew "the volcano was loose."

The Catastrophic Event

[NOTE: Amanda was born in 1895. Starting at the age of 17, she lived at the penitentiary with her parents and took an active part in the functioning of the prison, serving at times as her father's secretary and performing various other duties. It is said that she always carried a pistol with her in the penitentiary. In 1916, while she was a coed at The Ohio State University, her father put her in charge of the penitentiary for several days while he attended a convention in Kansas. She is credited as being the first woman to serve as the warden of a state penitentiary in the history of the United States. She was sometimes interviewed by the press as an unofficial spokesperson for the penitentiary, and once testified before the grand jury concerning the Ohio parole system. After the fire she was given the job of prison mail clerk and censor.

Much later in life, in 1962, long after leaving corrections work, she was elected as State Regent of the Ohio Society of the Daughters of the American Revolution, and three years later, became the Organizing Secretary-General of the National Society of the Daughters of the American Revolution. She died in 1985.]

Deputy Warden Woodard saw the fire as he was coming down Dennison Ave toward the penitentiary to report for duty. He saw the warden outside the walls near the Spring St. and Dennison Ave. stockade gate and had a conversation with him. The warden directed him to go in and take charge inside while he directed the efforts to prevent escape from outside. Woodard first went to the G&H Cellblock to confirm that the prisoners were being released. He then ordered that the prisoners in the E&F Dormitory, which adjoined the G&H Cellblock, be released. Then he went to the guardroom and got the keys to A&B and C&D Cellblocks, and

The Catastrophic Event

released those prisoners from their cells except the ones in Company K, "the bad-boy company." He told the "bad boys" that the fire wasn't a threat to them and promised to return and release them if it became a threat. Cellblocks A&B and C&D were referred to by prisoners and officials as "White City" because the interior of the building in which they were located had been painted white.

As the evening went on, the sidewalks became clogged with onlookers. The police kept the traffic lanes open to enable fire equipment to get to the penitentiary. The military troops managed the crowd of onlookers who had gathered. In order to move spectators to a safe distance from the walls, military personnel fixed bayonets to their rifles and marched around the perimeter of the prison, moving the people back and establishing boundaries for people to stay behind. Soldiers were posted along the way to enforce the boundaries set.

The fire raged for two hours before mostly burning itself out around 7:30 p.m. It was not officially declared to be under control until 9:00 p.m.

Guard William Baldwin
Courtesy of the Ohio History Connection

Guard Thomas Little
Courtesy of the Ohio History Connection

The Catastrophic Event

There was a delay in unlocking the cells to enable prisoners to get away from the fire. It was necessary to open a gate to have access to the cells in all the ranges in G&H Cellblock except those on the ground level. The delay occurred because Guard Thomas Watkinson, who was in charge of the G&H Cellblock during the day shift, had the key to the gate leading to the upper tiers and refused to open it. Little and Baldwin had the keys to the cells, but Watkinson had the gate key. Guards worked 12-hour shifts. The day shift started at 6:00 a.m. and ended at 6:00 p.m., when the night shift guards took over. Watkinson was the day shift guard for G&H Cellblock. Little and Baldwin were the night guards for that cellblock. The shift had not changed yet, so Watkinson was still responsible for the detention of the prisoners, and felt he needed orders from an officer to let the prisoners out. At that time the fire didn't seem to be life threatening.

Captain John Hall
Courtesy of the Columbus Dispatch

John Hall was the night shift captain of the guards and had arrived a little early to start his shift. According to the rules at the penitentiary, guard captains could give orders even though their shift hadn't begun. Guards were required to follow those orders.

Captain Hall left the guardroom to go to the G&H Cellblock (250 feet away) at the same time as Little and Baldwin, but arrived a few seconds

The Catastrophic Event

later. When Little arrived and told Watkinson to open the gate so they could let the prisoners out, Watkinson said he needed orders from someone with a higher rank than Little's. Little and Baldwin had the same rank as Watkinson. When Captain Hall arrived a few seconds later, he ordered Watkinson to "wait awhile" before letting the prisoners out. (The fire did not seem life threatening at the time.) Captain Hall ordered the building's windows opened (or broken) to allow for more ventilation in order to give the prisoners some relief from the smoke in the cellblock. After giving that order, Hall left the area where Watkinson was stationed to assess the seriousness of the fire and to get the windows opened. He didn't return.

[NOTE: Captain John Hall was 71 at the time of the fire. He had been working at the penitentiary for 21 years and had been captain of the night guards for 17 years.]

When they were refused the gate key, Little and Baldwin went to the cells on the ground-level, the only cells they had access to, and released the prisoners from those cells. After unlocking the ground-level cells, Little returned to Watkinson and demanded the key to the upper tiers. Watkinson again refused. While the prisoners yelled, "Open the goddamned doors!" and Guard Baldwin shouted, "Isn't this Hell!" Little took the key from Watkinson. Watkinson didn't resist. Little opened the gate and he and Baldwin then started releasing prisoners from the higher tiers. When Little and Baldwin got through the gate and began opening cells on the higher tiers, it was around 5:50 p.m.

During the period of the delay in getting the gate opened, the fire in the area of the G&H Cellblock grew, the heat intensified, and

The Catastrophic Event

the black smoke thickened and filled the cells. Due to the laws of physics and the location of the fire, the conditions were worse in the cells on the higher tiers.

Little and Baldwin's original plan was to release the prisoners on the sixth tier first and work their way down, but they were unable to get to the upper tiers because of the heat, so they started at the second tier and worked their way up as quickly as they could. They estimated that the difficulty in getting the key to the gate delayed their rescue plan by five to ten minutes.

Picture Taken from the top of a building on the west side of Dennison Avenue
Courtesy of the Ohio History Connection

Little released the prisoners from the "H" section (the west side of the cellblock) and Baldwin from the "G" section (the east side). Some of the prisoners released stayed inside the building instead of going to the prison yard and went with Little and Baldwin to help in the effort to get others out. Some firemen and other guards joined in the effort.

Since there were 34 cells per tier and there were four prisoners housed in each cell, the total number of men to be freed from the

The Catastrophic Event

cells on each tier was (34x4=) 136. Thus, it took a while to completely vacate each tier, especially since some prisoners had to be carried out.

There was a stiff breeze blowing from the northwest, and when fire breached the roof at the north end of the building, the wind got inside the building and accelerated the speed by which the fire spread south toward G&H Cellblock. By the time the rescuers began clearing the third level, the roof fire had spread south and was above the north end of Cellblock G&H, rapidly moving southward, roasting the prisoners on the upper levels as it went.

Some of the prisoners on the third level and many on the fourth level were in bad shape and had to be carried to the prison yard by prisoners who were in better condition and by Columbus firemen and guards.

The top of I&K Cellblock after the fire
Courtesy of the Ohio History Connection

By the time the fourth range was emptied, it was about 6:10 p.m. Little was overcome by smoke and collapsed after he had unlocked the last cell of the range on the fourth tier in the "H" section. Prisoners carried him out of the building. Baldwin made it to the

The Catastrophic Event

fifth tier of the "G" section, but collapsed there and was also carried out by prisoners.

The remaining rescuers, mostly prisoners, continued to the fifth tier, where things were far worse than below. The roof was on fire above those cells, and the heat was extreme. The rescuers encountered grisly sights of dead men lying face down on the floor clutching the bars. Others were lying dead on their bunks and some, under their bunks. The position of bodies showed that many convicts had turned toward the wall in futile efforts to protect their faces and eyes from the heat and smoke. Pillows had been stuffed in vents to attempt to keep out the smoke. Some prisoners had covered their heads with wet blankets. Some had their heads in their toilet or sink.

To make matters worse, the keys wouldn't open some of the cells. The locks were jammed because of the heat. Guards, inmates, and firemen had to use axes and sledge hammers to smash those locks. Only 13 of the 136 convicts on the fifth tier survived.

On the sixth tier things were worse still. The "would be" rescuers didn't reach the sixth tier until the fire was past its peak intensity. They encountered the same grisly sites as on the fifth tier and, in addition, some of the bedding and clothing in those cells were on fire. There was no hope of saving any of those men. All 136 prisoners on the sixth tier were dead, but the "would-be-rescuers" pressed on and removed the bodies. Some bodies were carried down the stairs, and some were lowered from tier to tier with ropes handled by prisoners, guards and firemen. At 6:40 p.m., the roof over the G&H Cellblock collapsed, and pieces of slate and burning wood came raining down in New Hall on the

The Catastrophic Event

convicts who were removing bodies.

Many prisoners were heroic in their efforts to save their fellow inmates; some died in the process. Big Jim Morton, a bank robber known as one of Ohio's most desperate criminals carried seven prisoners to safety and then brought out two corpses.

It was reported that "Wild Bill" Croningen, another dangerous criminal, carried 12 men out and went back to get more, but collapsed. Lying on the floor, he said, "I've done my part," and then died. These are but two of many heroic stories that were reported.

A cell on the 6th tier after the fire
Courtesy of the Ohio History Connection

When inspections were made after the fire was out, the smoke had cleared, and things had cooled off, the inspectors found half eaten candy, unopened letters, checker boards, and water-soaked books giving evidence that after dinner the unsuspecting prisoners on the various tiers had settled in for a quiet evening, when death swept in. The inspectors also found concrete walls of cells on tiers five and six that were burned white like the inside of an oven. They also found charred wooden items inside the cells on the sixth tier.

The Catastrophic Event

In the opinion of Fire Chief Nice, the delay in getting the prisoners cells opened so the men could flee from the fire was one of the main causes of the great loss of life.

Fireman first tried to fight the fire from outside.
Courtesy of the Ohio History Connection

One-hundred and forty firemen, using eight fire trucks and twenty-three hoses, fought the fire. The firemen's first attempt to deal with it was to direct a stream of water from a turret nozzle into the north window of I&K Cellblock. However, the heavy iron grilling in the window caused the stream to be so broken up as to render it ineffective.

Then a hose was run into New Hall through a door midway along the east side of the building leading to the prison yard and a stream was directed toward the I&K Cellblock, but by that time the fire was so fierce that the firemen couldn't get close to it, and the roof over I&K Cellblock had fallen in.

The top of G&H Cellblock after the fire
Courtesy of the Ohio History Connection

The Catastrophic Event

There were convicts in New Hall milling around who understood the plight of the prisoners in the cells on the upper tiers of G&H Cellblock and desperately wanted the firemen to concentrate their efforts there. Frustrated by their inability to get the firemen to understand that it was critical that it be done immediately, the convicts wrested the hose from the firemen and attempted to use it themselves, apparently thinking they could do better than the firemen. They directed the hose toward the fifth and sixth tiers, but the water pressure was insufficient and the hose was too short for the stream to reach it. They were soon persuaded to give the hose back to the firemen, but one angry prisoner cut the hose, rendering it useless. The firemen eventually ran hoses the entire length of the fifth and sixth ranges of G&H Cellblock and sprayed water into the cells, but it was too late.

By that time the fire was threatening the E&F Dormitory, which was next to G&H Cellblock, and the firemen turned their efforts toward stopping the fire before it destroyed that cell house. They cut holes in its roof, inserted hoses, and successfully stopped the fire from spreading beyond the G&H Cellblock.

Panic, Pain, Suffering, and Death

During the period of time when the cells were being opened so the prisoners could get away from the fire, terror and panic reigned. Frequent screams and hideous shrieks from helpless prisoners begging to be released were heard by the rescuers. Convicts on the upper two tiers wildly waved their arms, pounded on the bars, screamed, swore, prayed, and then were quieted by death—almost all of them. Dreading the prospect of being burned

The Catastrophic Event

to death, some on the upper tiers begged for someone to come up and shoot them. One convict on the sixth tier chose to slit his throat rather than die by fire.

One prisoner who was known and well-liked by other prisoners and guards for his sense of humor, shouted to his fellow inmates from his cell on the sixth tier as the fire was approaching, that a cop had once told him that someday he would be "cooked at the Ohio pen." Being broiled that day by a fire that was only a foot above the top of his cell was his fate and the fate of the others on the top tier.

A prisoner housed on the fourth tier recounted his experience as follows: "You can't imagine the horror of it! The fire swept up like some charging monster. It was upon us before we scarcely realized what was happening, and it got blistering hot. There were four of us in our cell. It got hot as hell, and we were scared. We started shouting to be released. We yelled and yelled for the guards to let us out, but they wouldn't. When it seemed that we would be roasted alive, we opened the water tap in our cell wide open, and as the floor became flooded, we lay down in the water and rolled around listening to other prisoners in the burning cellblock screaming. We put our faces in the water and dashed water over each other. We kept this up until, at last, a couple of prisoners came along and got us out."

Another prisoner pointed to a cell on the sixth tier and said, "There is where my brother died. Yep, Hank died in there like a rat. He never had a chance." Inside the cell he pointed to a couple of charred wooden objects, "There is what is left of his radio, and there is the box where he kept his stuff." He turned away and continued, "I did my best to reach him when they released me from my cell in White City, but I couldn't get near this place."

Water-soaked and scorched, partially written notes to loved ones telling them of the situation and saying good-bye were found in prisoners' cells.

One dead convict had a note pinned to his shirt as to who should be notified of his death.

Outside in the prison yard, located on the east side of New Hall, blankets were laid on the ground, and the injured and dead were carried out through a door in the east wall of New Hall and laid on the blankets. Efforts to help them were made. If a prisoner showed signs of life, he was carried into the prison hospital. If he was obviously dead, he was left on the blanket. Groans and words of encouragement passed between the injured and the men who were helping. A seared face, lack of breathing, and silence from a victim were the signs that he was dead. Moaning meant the prisoner was alive. As the evening wore on and the rescuers were clearing the higher ranges, there was less and less moaning from the prisoners

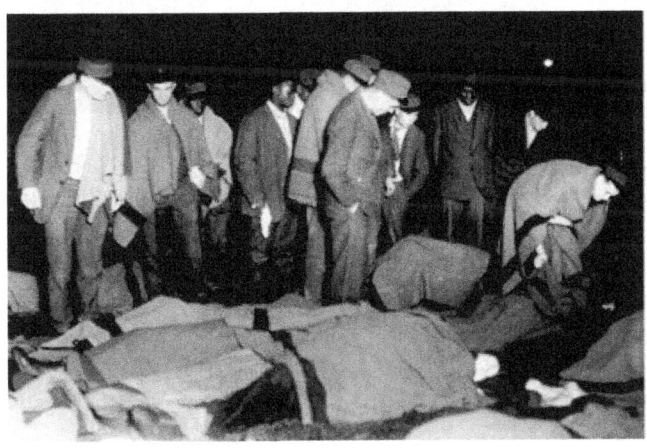

Prisoners identifying their dead comrades
Courtesy of the Ohio History Connection

The Catastrophic Event

brought out.

Before the rescue efforts had ended, the ground had become a quagmire because of previous rains and the water from the firemen's hoses. The rescue efforts continued long after nightfall. After checking the prisoner carried out and taking him to the hospital if he was alive, the rescuers returned for other prisoners, stumbling in the dark over bodies on their way. Some fell headfirst into the slimy mud.

Smoke filled the air, and occasionally a flame was visible. The shadows from magnesium flares used for providing some light in the prison yard added a surreal atmosphere. Lanterns threw ghastly light on the faces of the dead convicts as guards were recording the numbers stenciled on their clothing to identify them. Convicts who were

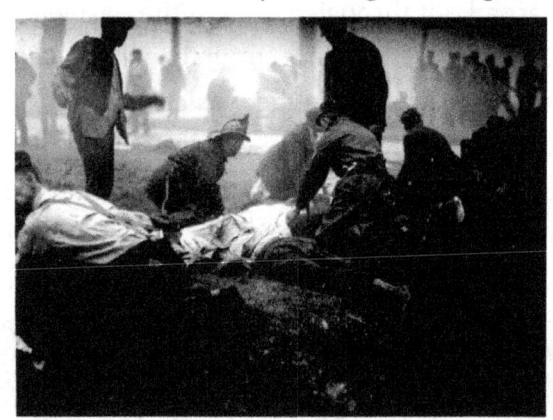
Prisoners and a fireman attending to injured convicts
Courtesy of the Ohio History Connection

still able to walk and who were not involved in helping other prisoners wandered about as if in a daze, scantily clad and wet, shivering in the cool damp evening air, and having only coffee to comfort them. Some ranted and raved because they were crazed by the horrible ordeal they had just gone through.

Outside the burning building, as inside, the situation got more and more horrible as the rescuers reached the upper tiers. Doctors and clergymen poured into the yard from the hospital. The doctors looked for live prisoners to treat as priests administered the last rites to those who were dying. The yard resembled a battlefield strewn with corpses.

Dead prisoners in the prison yard
Courtesy of the Ohio History Connection

The total casualties from the fire were 320 killed and over 200 hospitalized. Only a small portion of the dead men were actually burned—most died from the intense heat or from lack of oxygen due to the smoke and fumes.

Help Given

Shortly after the fire started, doctors and nurses began arriving at the penitentiary to administer first aid. They came from all over Central Ohio, including from local hospitals, Grant, White Cross, Mt. Carmel, Mercy, St. Anthony, University, and St. Francis. Hospitals also sent supplies and cots. Medical help arrived at the penitentiary very quickly due to the efforts of Elizabeth Sampson, Director of the Physicians and Surgeons Bureau who, with help from her sister and another lady, spread the word to the doctors and hospitals in the Central Ohio area of the need for medical services and supplies at the penitentiary. She was acting in response to the following message received from Warden Thomas's office: "We need every physician in Franklin County here at once. For the sake of humanity, find them. Send them in." She secured three open lines from the phone company, and in one hour ferreted out 130 physicians and dispatched them to the penitentiary, shouting to them: "To the pen, to the pen—men trapped and burning to death." Through the evening, she continued finding doctors and sending them to the prison. By 9:00 p.m., there was almost a doctor for every patient. Eventually, nurses who arrived to help were turned away by order of the warden because of his concern for their safety.

Elizabeth Sampson
Courtesy of the Columbus Dispatch

The prison hospital had 180 beds, 147 of which were already being used by prisoners who were sick before the fire. Those patients who were able gave up their beds for the fire victims. Cots were also set up.

The Catastrophic Event

Many of those who were carried into the hospital were pronounced dead on arrival or died at the hospital shortly after arriving and were carried back out to the yard and were lined up with the rest of the dead. A physician described the stream of human forms at the door of the prison hospital as follows: "Those going in are believed to be alive, those coming out are dead."

Prisoners asked doctors, reporters, firemen and others to please notify their loved ones that they were alive. One frantic prisoner who had heard over a radio that he was listed as one of the dead begged a reporter to notify his mother that he was OK. (Mistakes were made in identifying the dead because some prisoners were wearing shirts belonging to other prisoners, and identification was done by recording the number stenciled on the victim's shirt.)

After the fire had burned out, a telegraph machine was set up in the deputy warden's office so convicts could notify relatives that they were safe. Five hundred telegrams had been sent out by midnight.

One convict asked a policeman to send a telegram to his folks telling them that he was all right. The policeman asked, "How about saying "Escaped. OK." The prisoner replied, "No, they might misunderstand that. Better say: "Big fire here. Not hurt."

For the first time in history, the nation was kept informed of an on-going disaster by radio broadcasts. News of the fire was flashed to the 28 stations of the Columbia Broadcasting System. The flashes originated at the Columbus radio station, WAIU, which was at that time part of the CBS network.

[NOTE: WAIU was owned by the American Insurance Union, the original owner of the AIU Building, the tallest building in Columbus at the time—now called the "Leveque Tower." WAIU was headquartered in the AIU building, and its signal was broadcast from there. In the 1930s, WAIU was renamed WHKC and in 1954 became known as WTVN.]

WAIU made a direct connection by telephone with the penitentiary and began broadcasting information about the

Otto (Deacon) Gardner
Courtesy of the Columbus Dispatch

fire shortly after 6:00 p.m. Besides information regarding the progress of the fire, the news flashes included calls for medical supplies and cots as well as messages directed to members of the Ohio National Guard to report for duty. In many homes, families gathered around the radio to hear about the fire and listened throughout the evening.

At first, the broadcasting was done by members of the staff of WAIU, Columbus newspaper reporters, and various physicians

The Catastrophic Event

who had cared for injured prisoners. Starting at 8:30 p.m., Otto Gardner, a prisoner, became one of the broadcasters. Gardner was a convicted murderer serving a life sentence for shooting his wife and another woman on a street car. Gardner, whose prison nickname was Deacon, gave the nation a graphic radio picture of the tragedy as it unfolded. William Paley, president of CBS, sent Gardner a check for $500 as a thank you for his good work.

Later in the evening another prisoner reported the names of prisoners who had died in the fire. Other prisoners broadcast short messages for their loved ones and requested listeners to forward the messages. "I'm OK.", "Escaped without injury.", and "Tell mother I'm all right." were typical messages. Names and street addresses of the intended recipients were given.

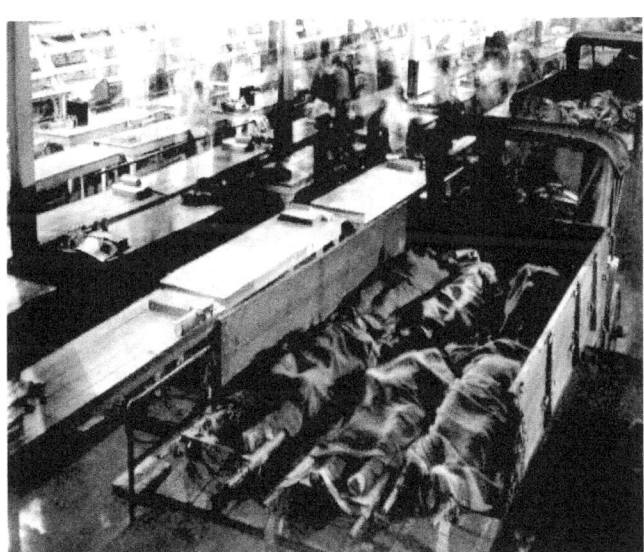

Trucks taking bodies to fairgrounds
Courtesy of the Ohio History Connection

Shortly before midnight the process of taking the dead to a makeshift morgue at the fairgrounds began. The warden's daughter, Amanda, was in charge of overseeing the removal of the bodies. They were taken to the fairgrounds in army trucks—six to a truck—where nearly 100 Central Ohio embalmers under the direction of funeral director Carroll Weir, worked through the night and all day Tuesday, preparing the victims for burial. The last bodies were removed from the penitentiary at 4:15 a.m.

Many poignant stories were told concerning the victims of the fire. One concerned a young man who stole a car in order to sell it so he could use the money to get married to "the only love of his life." Instead, he was convicted of car theft and sent to the penitentiary. His nickname in prison was "Bridegroom." He was scheduled to be released from prison in May. He had a job lined up, and he and the girl had plans to marry as soon as he was out. He died in the fire.

There was a prisoner housed in G&H Cellblock who had a younger brother in the cellblock. After the older brother got out, he went back in and carried several convicts out. Then he went back in and carried his younger brother out, but he was dead.

Corpses at the fairgrounds
Courtesy of the Ohio History Connection

The Catastrophic Event

There were four brothers who were prisoners at the penitentiary at the time of the fire and all were housed in the G&H Cellblock. Two died; two lived.

Shock And Anger

Shock and anger characterized the reaction of the surviving convicts. At the prison hospital, a convict complained to a priest, "Father, we are human, why should we have to die like caged rats?"

In response to someone who compared the tragedy to the World War, a prisoner said, "The war! Don't try to tell me this was like the war! I saw both, brother. Over there, we had a chance for our lives. We could run if we couldn't fight, but not here. Here, there was nothing for these guys to do but go crazy, locked inside a box while they watched the fire coming after them. They screamed for God to open those damned doors, and when the doors didn't open, all that was left was to stand and let the fire burn the meat off and hope it wouldn't be long about it."

Some convicts were driven mad by the horror of what they experienced. One prisoner with an arm that had been rendered useless by wounds in the World War had to have his good arm tied down because he was out of control raving about the death of his cellmate.

The prisoners in the dormitories next to G&H Cellblock and most of those in the White City cellblocks were let out of their cells on the order of Deputy Warden Woodard because of the risk of the roof fire spreading to those buildings. That led to a great number of convicts being loose on the prison grounds, including many troublemakers housed in White City.

Many of the prisoners in White City were "idle prisoners," meaning that they didn't work, either because they refused to work, or because there was no work available for which they were suitable. The section of White City where they were housed was sometimes referred to as the "Idle House." Idle prisoners tend to be troublemakers because idleness breeds mischief, in accordance with the adage, "idleness is the devil's workshop." The worst troublemakers were assigned to "K Company," which was housed in White City. "K Company" was sometimes referred to as the "bad boy" company, and prisoners in "K Company" were referred to as the "red shirt gang" because they were required to wear red and white striped uniforms so they could easily be identified as potential troublemakers. The prisoners of "K Company" were not released.

Some of the prisoners set free within the prison walls on the night of the fire committed hostile acts toward the firefighters, including roughing up firemen, cutting a fire hose, throwing stones at fire trucks and firemen and in other ways interfering with the firemen's efforts to deal with the fire in New Hall.

Additional fires were set by convicts while New Hall burned, and prisoners interfered with firemen's efforts to put them out. The convicts set the prison's woolen and cotton mills on fire during the evening. One fireman, who was attempting to keep a group of prisoners from setting fire to the prison chapel, was injured by a rock thrown by a convict.

The Catastrophic Event

Another fireman was set upon by convicts when he attempted to put out a fire set by them in a wooden dormitory on the east side of the complex. He was grabbed by the throat and thrown out of the building. Prisoners threatened to kill another fireman who tried to put it out. Finally, a squad of firemen rushed into the dormitory assisted by guards and extinguished it.

The hooligans also attempted to set fire to a gasoline tank attached to a fire truck by throwing blankets under the tank and trying to set them on fire with matches. While they were attempting to light the blanket, a fireman, although threatened by the prisoners, drove the vehicle away from the blankets, thereby thwarting their plan.

Eventually the firemen threatened not to fight the fire any longer if they continued to be harassed and endangered by the unruly prisoners. Army troops with drawn bayonets were sent in to protect the firemen.

Guards dealing with the hostile convicts were disarmed before going inside the prison to eliminate any possibility of prisoners getting their weapons.

Prisoners yelled, "burn the screws (guards)." In the dining hall tables were upset and dishes were broken. Threats to kill the warden were made.

Troublemakers gathered in groups threatening more trouble. All available lawmen from the sheriff's office and the Columbus Police Department were summoned to the penitentiary. Flood lights brought to the penitentiary from the Olentangy Park

The Catastrophic Event

Swimming Pool were mounted on the Spring Street wall, illuminating the entire yard.

After a time, the groups of troublemakers thinned out, and the convicts went to their cell houses; however, many of them stayed up all night.

The Board of Inquiry

The Board of Inquiry

Ohio's governor, Myers Cooper, was out of the state at the time of the fire. When he learned of it, he immediately headed back to Columbus. At 4:00 a.m. on April 22, he directed Ohio Director of Welfare Hal Griswold to begin an inquiry into the facts surrounding the disaster for the purpose of trying to determine the cause of the fire and why there were delays in sending a fire alarm and releasing the prisoners. He also wanted to know what precautions were taken to prevent such catastrophes. Shortly afterward he directed Ohio Attorney General Gilbert Bettman to assist Griswold.

However, John J. Chester, the prosecutor of Franklin County, the county in which the penitentiary was situated, went to the prison during the night of the fire and mingled with the prisoners, gathering information, and at 5:30 on the morning of Tuesday, April 22, the day after the fire, he began an investigation on behalf of his office, by questioning the warden in the administrative offices of the penitentiary. The interrogation was heated. Chester accused Thomas of being responsible for the great loss of life and said that he should step aside as warden until his investigation was completed. Warden Thomas refused.

Governor Cooper arrived at the penitentiary at 7:30 a.m., and turned the inquiry that was started by Chester over to the attorney general. A county prosecutor has authority to investigate an event occurring in his county where a crime might have been committed, but the governor, by directing that an investigation be made by the attorney general, preempted Chester's effort. At the governor's request, Chester continued to be involved in the inquiry, but the attorney general was in charge.

The Board of Inquiry

The members of the governor's Board of Inquiry first toured the G&H Cellblock and then, at 10:00 a.m., began hearing testimony. The governor attended the morning session of the inquiry. Earl Shively, the first assistant attorney general, did the questioning that day.

The Board of Inquiry meeting in the penitentiary's administrative offices -- At the Far right is Warden Thomas, seated next to him is Governor Cooper, and on the far left is Prosecutor Chester
Courtesy of the Dailey Archives

The Governor's inquiry continued for five days. During the inquiry, forty-four witnesses were questioned concerning the fire, including the warden, guards, other prison officials, Columbus officials, and several prisoners. The transcript of the proceedings contained 727 pages of testimony. In addition, New Hall and the G&H Cellblock were inspected twice by the board members.

Testimony was received supporting the facts given in the previous section entitled "Fire." However, conflicting testimony was given concerning the delay in getting the prisoners out of their cells. Neither Hall nor Watkinson was willing to accept responsibility for the delay.

The Board of Inquiry

Watkinson testified at the inquiry that, although he had the key necessary for Guards Little and Baldwin to have access to the upper tiers, he had been ordered by Captain John Hall to "wait awhile" before letting the prisoners out. Because of his rank, Hall had authority over him, and Hall never changed the order.

Captain Hall's testimony was vague. He did not admit to intentionally delaying the release of the prisoners from their cells.

[NOTE: Both Hall and Watkinson would have realized that it was likely the fire had been set by prisoners to facilitate a mass escape. They knew the stockade gates would be opened to admit fire trucks and the gates might be overrun by the inmates and also fire truck ladders might be seized by prisoners and used to go over the walls. They were also aware that arrangements had been made for the police, the National Guard, and Regular Army troops to come to the prison to help prevent escapes. Either, or both, of them might have felt it would be best to delay opening the cells to give the police and military personnel time to arrive, so long as it didn't endanger the prisoners' lives.

Life-threatening fires don't normally occur in concrete and steel cellblocks inside brick and stone buildings where the only flammable materials are the prisoners' clothing and bedding. Fires occasionally happen in such cellblocks when a convict sets a mattress on fire, accidentally or intentionally, but that kind of fire is not serious and is quickly doused by a bucket brigade of convicts and guards. Furthermore, the fire was at the north end of I&K Cellblock, more than 185 feet from the nearest prisoner in G&H Cellblock, with only an unoccupied, partially completed, steel and concrete cellblock in between.

The Board of Inquiry

If those were the thoughts that led to the delay, there was a tragic failure to comprehend the danger posed by the oil soaked wooden forms and the other lumber high up on the north end of cellblock I&K and the strong wind blowing from the northwest. They failed to foresee the roof catching fire in the construction area and the fire quickly spreading to the part of the roof above the occupied cellblock.]

The warden testified that because he had heard that Guard Watkinson had refused to give the gate key to Guards Little and Baldwin, he suspended Watkinson when he came to work on Tuesday morning at 6:00 a.m. and ordered him to stay out of the prison for his own safety.

Columbus Fire Chief A. E. Nice testified at the inquiry that the first fire alarm was "pulled from a city box" located on Dennison Avenue, at its intersection with Dublin Avenue, at 5:39 p.m. Further testimony established that the alarm was turned in by a trusty, Howard Miller, the prison's chauffeur, who was returning from an errand. He was driving south on Dennison Avenue alongside the prison and was slowed down by an automobile accident ahead of him. He noticed the smoke, stopped his car, got out, and turned in the alarm. The first alarm received from inside the penitentiary was at 5:40. The fire department arrived a few minutes after receiving the first alarm. At 5:42 p.m., a second alarm was sent by Assistant Fire Chief C. W. Ogborn, who had arrived at the prison in response to the first alarm. At 5:46 p.m., he turned in a third alarm. Chief Nice arrived on the scene about 5:58 p.m. and turned in a fourth alarm at 6:03 p.m.

Fire Chief Nice testified that in his opinion the delay in turning in a fire alarm (from shortly after 5:30 p.m., when the smoke was seen and reported to the guardroom by Guard Whetstone from the tower on Spring Street and also reported by Guard Light to the guardroom at about the same time, to 5:39 p.m., when the first alarm was sent) as being one of the major causes for the great loss of life. Chief Nice testified that the delay in getting the prisoners out of their cells was the other main cause.

Testimony to the board established that no standing instructions had been issued to guards regarding what they should do in the event of a fire. The warden said that it was understood that all should use common sense and good judgment in whatever occurred. "You cannot make rules to cover every detail of an emergency," he said. It was also established that no fire drills had been conducted at the prison and that the only equipment for fighting fires, a two-wheeled cart with a hose attached, had been discarded.

As stated above, Warden Thomas testified that as soon as he was notified of the fire at 5:35 p.m., he went to the guardroom. At the guardroom, in answer to his query, he was told that a fire alarm had been turned in. He ordered that an alarm be sent again. He instructed Guards Little and Baldwin, who were in the guardroom at the time, to take the keys to G&H Cellblock so the prisoners could be let out. He also ordered that keys be taken to the stockade gates to admit fire trucks. The warden then went outside the walls to oversee efforts to prevent prisoners from escaping. He didn't go back inside the walls that evening.

Warden Thomas testified that he was highly suspicious the fire had been set by a group of prisoners for the purpose of facilitating

The Board of Inquiry

a prison break in the chaos that would ensue and that the prisoners would probably attempt to take him captive as a way of advancing their escape plan. He further testified that his responsibility, after seeing to it that a fire alarm had been sent and sending the keys to G&H Cellblock so the prisoners could be released, was to stay out of the reach of the prisoners and to do everything possible to prevent escapes. He made the following statement:

"Since the recent riot at Auburn State Penitentiary, I have received numerous authentic reports from inside the walls that the men were organizing to stage a similar demonstration here. In fact, the situation had become so acute I had made arrangements with the National Guard at Fort Hayes and with the Columbus police department to be in readiness for any emergencies here. The convicts have been planning and brooding since the Auburn State Penitentiary outbreak."

[NOTE: On December 11, 1929, inmates at Auburn State Penitentiary in New York rioted, killing one guard and taking the warden and seven other guards hostage. They demanded safe passage from the prison and barricaded themselves in the main hall. Troopers and an Army National Guard detail stormed the hall freeing the warden and four guards. Eight inmates were killed. The remaining rioters fled to a cellblock, continuing to shoot and use teargas against the troopers. The next morning, their ringleader was shot and killed and the rest of the rioters were subdued, thus ending the riot. The New York troopers remained on guard duty at the prison until April 1, 1930, only three weeks before the Ohio Penitentiary fire.

The Board of Inquiry

Over the nine-month period preceding the Ohio Penitentiary fire, there had been a series of prison disturbances around the nation, resulting in 20 deaths. The first occurred at Clinton Prison in Dannemora, N. Y. where two prisoners were killed and six wounded. Very shortly after that there was a riot at Auburn Prison, N. Y. where two prisoners were killed and 12 people were wounded, including three guards who were shot. Four days later a riot occurred at Leavenworth; one prisoner was killed and three were wounded. Then on October 3, 1930, at the Colorado State Penitentiary, ten guards were taken hostage and four were shot and killed. Two months later a second outbreak occurred at Auburn Prison, N. Y. (described above). In March 1930, a riot occurred at the state prison at Jefferson City, Missouri. Just two days before the Ohio Penitentiary fire, on Saturday, April 19, 1930, two convicts were killed and two others injured and a prison guard critically wounded at the Rhode Island State Prison at Cranston, R. I.]

The warden pointed to the following as support for his suspicion that the Easter Monday fire had been set by prisoners:

An inmate told him on Sunday night, the night before the fire, that another prisoner had said to him, "this place will soon be a blazing inferno."

A guard told him that on the night of the fire, he heard a prisoner say, "Well the spark hit in the right place this time."

He had received a letter informing him that the writer of the letter had heard from a recently released prisoner that a small group of inmates had been stealing an inflammable liquid over

The Board of Inquiry

the last several months preparing for a fire.

Another recently released prisoner had informed him that he had heard of an escape plot while he was incarcerated at the penitentiary and that the attempt had been delayed for some reason.

A letter from an undertaker had been received by him stating that the father of an inmate who died in the fire told the undertaker he had been informed by his son that something awful was going to happen at the penitentiary.

Prisoners who testified bitterly denounced Captain Hall's failure to order the range gate opened in G&H Cellblock and characterized him as the most despised man at the prison. Several prisoners testified that they heard Captain Hall say not to let the prisoners out, just "open the windows."

Prisoners also denounced Warden Thomas, claiming that he allowed brutality by guards against prisoners, and they demanded his removal.

In response to the prisoners' demand, Attorney General Bettman recommended to the governor that Warden Thomas be temporarily suspended. Warden Thomas reacted to the attorney general's recommendation by saying that the demand was not from the majority of the prisoners, but from the 10% rebellious element and that his removal would be giving up regularly constituted government to the demands of rebellious prisoners.

For the first three days, the Board of Inquiry heard testimony in the administrative offices of the penitentiary below the quarters

The Board of Inquiry

of the warden. On Friday, April 25, Attorney General Bettman moved the investigation to his office. Bettman planned to close the investigation at the end of that day's proceedings. However, at the request of Warden Thomas, Bettman agreed to hear additional testimony on the following day, Saturday, April 26.

Warden Thomas, having read the transcript of the testimony given to the Board of Inquiry up to that point, wanted to offer additional testimony for the record to clarify and rebut testimony given by some witnesses. Although many letters had been received supporting and praising the warden in the actions he had taken, he felt that the testimony of some of the prisoners and others may have made an impression on some that he was an uncaring, brutal, negligent, and cowardly villain. He wanted an opportunity to refute that.

When Attorney General Bettman opened the inquiry on Saturday, April 26, Warden Thomas was represented by his son, Donald Thomas, a lawyer and a former Dayton Municipal Court Judge. His son presented witnesses to refute testimony previously given that was unfavorable to his father.

Then the warden took the stand and told the board that for 17 years he had unsuccessfully asked the legislature for funding of projects to alleviate the overcrowded conditions at the prison and to construct fireproof buildings. He testified as follows:

"I have called their attention repeatedly to the fire traps, and they would say: 'Yes, warden, we know you're telling the truth. We know you need it.' Then they would walk away and forget about it."

The Board of Inquiry

"While striving, on the one hand, to get money out of the legislature and, on the other, being obliged to stuff 4,200 prisoners in an institution originally meant to house 1,500, I have been faced always by the ominous possibility of prison riot and escape."

"In 1913, the year I became warden, I was called in by Governor Cox to talk the penitentiary situation over. Governor Cox said he wanted the best prison in the world, and I said it couldn't be had with the buildings on hand but that I would do the best I could."

"At the time, a prison commission was appointed to select a new prison site. London Prison Farm resulted. Work was commenced and then stopped while a legislative committee investigated and reported back. It reported back that the prison couldn't be built using prison labor and work stopped. But it has been built using prison labor and on the very same foundation that was started and stopped, and it has been built without a disturbance, thus disproving the legislature."

"At each legislative session, I have importuned for help. For 12 years I received nothing, then the last few years when it was seen that it was absolutely necessary, the legislature has granted some relief in housing facilities."

"I have always been against building anything but fireproof buildings. I protested when the (wooden) dormitory was built at the Junction City brick plant. I said that to build a wooden dormitory at a brick plant reminded me of the story of the shoemaker whose children all went barefooted. That wooden construction resulted in a holocaust in which nine lives were lost."

"Repeatedly, I made recommendations for more space and more prisons. And what happened?"

"In 1921, the legislature passed laws which gave judges the right to fix minimum sentences and increased the minimum sentence for robbery from 1 to 15 years to 10 to 25 years. I told them the laws would just fill the prisons and not stop crime but that since they had passed the laws, we would have to have more buildings."

"That year the population of the penitentiary, including the London prison farm, was 2037; now, including the farm and the brick plants, it is nearly 6,000."

"I have recommended a prison be built especially for the unfit. By that, I mean the physically unfit as well as the mentally unfit—the psychopaths and the attitudinally unfit. And, it is the latter class—the attitudinally unfit—which is causing all the trouble today."

"As a further relief measure, I have gone before the last two legislatures with bills providing classification of prisoners. The bills were passed in the Senate but defeated in the House, because so much pressure was brought from the outside."

"One attorney general ruled one way on the minimum sentence question, holding that prisoners could be released when the minimum sentence prescribed by the statute expired. The next attorney general reversed him and held that the prisoners had to serve until the minimum sentence fixed by the judge expired. So I held many men in the penitentiary who otherwise would have been free. And after I had done that, the courts ruled that the attorney general who last ruled was wrong, and those prisoners could have been out of the penitentiary all that time."

"Under the present system, a recommendation for pardon has to be made to the governor, and there seems to be some disposition of some on the outside to criticize pardons—saying that there are too many, regardless of the rights thereof."

"It might be of moment to say that at the last American Prison Association meeting in Toronto, it was voted that no prison should hold more than 1,200 men at a time. At the time of the fire, we had 4,200 men within the walls of Ohio Penitentiary."

"There seems to be some stress laid on fire drills in prisons. I have been attending prison congresses for 17 years, and I have never heard the matter broached. The purpose of fire drills is to produce an orderly procedure. You don't yell 'Fire!' because that would produce pandemonium. Now we actually have at Ohio penitentiary what corresponds to fire drills because three or four times a day, we march the men, in orderly platoon formation, in and out of the buildings."

"Then, there has been some stress and criticism about a fire department inside the penitentiary. I want to make that quite clear. We had an old wagon—with two wheels—that we tried to use, but it always made the city firemen angry. They said we were in their way, and they had to take our hose off and put theirs on. It simply impeded their work."

"The city fire department is only two squares from the penitentiary. We have timed them often, and it takes only about

The Board of Inquiry

two minutes for them to get into the prison after the alarm."

"We were forbidden by the city fire department to use its hydrants, and they made inspections to see that we didn't. We make a monthly fire equipment report to the department of public welfare. I now offer those reports as exhibits. You will note that they all say we depend on the city for protection."

"Then there has been something said about cruelty to prisoners."

"That's something that has not been practiced since I have been warden and something I will not stand for. I believe in good discipline, and I have had good discipline."

"I'll have to brand testimony of cruelty as absolutely false!"

"There were a few cases where the use of force was not sustained by evidence. Those officers were suspended—not for brutality, but for use of force where they had no right to do so."

"I have been criticized, too, for not being inside during the fire, and the question has been asked as to why I was on the outside."

"There are two persons in each state who should never be on the inside of a prison on such an occasion—the governor of the state and the warden of the penitentiary, because they are the two men who can order the gates opened, or, in prison phraseology, can 'take them out.' "

"Escapes at such times as this have been planned and plotted on a number of occasions."

"I cite you to the case of Warden Jennings of Auburn (N.Y.) prison.

The Board of Inquiry

The prisoners captured him, and I don't know what would have happened if it hadn't been for the troopers."

"I cite you, also, to the riot in the Colorado prison, where the warden was outside, but where the prisoners killed the guards on refusal of the warden to order the gates opened."

"In every prison there are always plots and schemes for 'delivery.' Some people seem to think prison is such a nice place that all the prisoners want to stay in. They want out! Some of them are desperate enough to go to any end to get out. Many times my attention has been called to plots, and I have been very watchful that they did not succeed."

"We search the ground every morning for guns that may have been thrown over the walls. We search for nitroglycerine. We have guards on the outside as well as those on the walls not only to keep prisoners from coming over the walls but to keep help from being given the prisoners from the outside. All gangsters today are not locked up."

"I might go on and describe to you our effort at uplift and encouragement, about our schools and the hundreds of graduates in correspondence courses we have, of the trades the men learn and of the writers we have turned out."

"I want to say at this time that my heart goes out to all those who lost loved ones in the fire. I have seen them coming here—wives and relations—every day. I have seen them come for 17 years. I've seen the misery on the outside."

"There's more suffering on the outside than there is on the inside.

By that I mean the families on the outside on this sad occasion make it a double tragedy for me."

Prior to his father giving his testimony the warden's son, Don Thomas, presented witnesses, including James Woodard, Deputy Warden of Ohio Penitentiary; T. C. Jenkins, Superintendent of the Mansfield Reformatory; and Sgt. Harry Hostetter, Sergeant of the guards at the Ohio Penitentiary.

Deputy Warden Woodard testified that he became deputy warden at the same time Thomas became warden, and they had served together in their respective capacities for 17 years; that he (Woodard) is in charge of prisoner discipline; that guards are allowed to hit prisoners with their hands if necessary to get the prisoner to obey, but if a guard resorts to hitting the prisoner with a club, it must be reported to him, and he holds "court" to decide if it was justified, and if he finds that it was not, the guard is disciplined; that he could recall only two instances during his seventeen years as deputy warden where he found that such discipline was not justified, and in both cases, the guard was suspended.

Mansfield Reformatory Superintendent Jenkins testified that in attending prison conferences he had come in contact with heads of penal institutions in various states, and he had never heard of any prisons that had fire drills.

Sgt. Hostetter testified that there had been frequent talk of a big penitentiary break. It was planned that prisoners would grab the warden and make him order the gate opened or slit his throat. He had heard of the plan several times and had heard of the plan as

The Board of Inquiry

recently as three weeks ago. He further testified that prison officials had decided that in the event of a disturbance, the warden was to stay out of reach of the prisoners and also that on the night of the fire, Columbus Police Chief French had advised Thomas not to go inside the walls.

At the end of the proceedings on Saturday, April 26, Bettman concluded the inquiry. He and the board then prepared a report on the matters investigated and delivered it to Governor Myers Cooper on Friday, May 2, 1930.

In regard to the origin of the fire, one of the possible causes considered by the board was that it started by spontaneous combustion. Although the theory was advanced, there was nothing to support it.

Another of the possible causes considered was that a blowtorch was left burning and started the fire. However, no such torch was found, and there was no evidence indicating that was the cause.

Another possibility advanced was that it was due to faulty temporary wiring used for lighting the construction project. Testimony revealed that permanent wiring had been installed on the lower four tiers of the I&K Cellblock, but the partially completed fifth tier was lighted from above by a temporary installation of three groups of five 40 watt bulbs mounted on boards suspended from wooden trusses, and some un-insulated electrical wires might have been used in rigging the temporary lighting. An inmate electrician was responsible for the installation. During the afternoon of the day of the fire, those lights went off three times. The lights were left on after the workday ended.

The Board of Inquiry

Attorney General Bettman's report was based on 727 pages of testimony given to the Board of Inquiry, by 44 witnesses over the five days immediately following the fire. The report stated that although it was impossible to determine positively the cause of the fire, strong circumstantial evidence pointed to defective temporary wiring in the construction area of the I&K Cellblock where the fire originated. It was the opinion of the board that the fire could have been prevented by switching off the current after working hours. The report blamed the loss of life on the lack of proper instructions as to what to do in case of such an emergency and the delay in turning in the alarm to the city fire department. The report's specific findings were 1) The temporary lighting was improper and dangerous and was the probable cause of the fire, 2) the current to the lights should have been turned off or a patrol of the I&K Cellblock construction site should have been maintained when construction work was not in progress at the site, 3) prison officials were negligent in not having an organized plan to deal with a fire in New Hall, and 4) the prison administration's rules failed to designate someone to be in command of situations in the absence of the warden.

The governor also received reports from State Fire Marshal Ray Gill, based on the investigation of Special Investigator Joseph Clear and Chief Assistant Fire Marshal Edward Lee. The report stated that Clear and Lee had dismissed the theory that the fire was caused by defective wiring since a guard reported the lights were still working at the time the fire started. The report also set forth various facts that had led them to believe the fire had been set by arsonists using an incendiary device. It stated they were continuing to investigate and felt certain that at a later date, they would be able to substantiate their theory.

A third report was received by the governor from the Ohio Inspection Bureau that concluded that the cause of the fire might never be known for certain, but was most likely incendiarism. It dismissed the theory that the fire resulted from defective wiring, having found no evidence to support it.

After studying the reports, the governor issued a statement in which he said that he did not accept the attorney general's theory that the fire was caused by faulty wiring. He stated that he would await the completion of the fire marshal's investigation before coming to a conclusion as to the cause.

The governor's statement also said he had been informed by Warden Thomas weeks before the fire that a concerted effort was afoot at the penitentiary to effect a wholesale riot and escape, the idea having been engendered following the Auburn, N. Y. prison fire and riot, and that the warden had made arrangements to have the National Guard in readiness in case of an uprising at the prison. In his statement, Governor Cooper called attention to the "ever-present threat and hazard beyond the possibility of fire that confronted officials at the penitentiary, namely, that of riot and wholesale escape." The governor suggested that this needed to be considered by ones who would blame the tragedy on negligence of prison officials.

The Rebellion Following the Fire

Tuesday, April 22, 1930

On Monday night the 1,300 convicts in White City (A&B and C&D Cellblocks, excepting "Company K") were released from their cells during the fire. They refused to be locked in after the fire was out and remained loose. About 300 of the surviving prisoners from Cellblock G&H (those who were not in the hospital) were being housed in the prison chapel where the doors didn't have locks. After the fire, the iron bars were taken off the windows of a wooden dormitory on the east side of the prison grounds which housed 800 prisoners, thereby making it possible for the prisoners to get out of the building. Therefore, at least 2,400 prisoners were essentially loose within the walls. Most prisoners went to bed, but as of 4:00 a.m. on Tuesday morning, 200 to 300 prisoners were still wandering around in the corridors of their cell house.

There was a rumor that there would be an attempt to break out at 6:00 a.m. Additional guardsmen were stationed and machine guns were mounted at the wagon stockade and railroad stockade gates, but 6:00 a.m. passed and there was no attempt to escape.

On Tuesday, the White City prisoners destroyed the locks on their cells, and on Tuesday night they refused to retire when they were told to do so at 9:00 p.m. Hundreds of convicts surrounded guards who were attempting to get them to retire. Eventually, the guards retreated without succeeding in getting them to their cells.

Wednesday, April 23, 1930

Sobbing mothers, wives and other relatives began the grisly process of identifying and claiming the corpses. A telegram had been sent from the penitentiary to families of deceased convicts notifying them of the death of their loved ones and giving them instructions for claiming the bodies. The bodies were in coffins in the Horticulture Building at the fairgrounds. Family members first went to the warden's office at the penitentiary and obtained a pass which they took to the Horticulture Building. The Red Cross was in charge at the fairgrounds, assisted by members of the Columbus Junior League. The family members waited outside until the body was located. Then they were taken to view the body.

Women at the prison to get passes to allow them to claim bodies
Courtesy of the Ohio History Connection

Some bodies were seared beyond recognition and had been identified by fingerprints. Three women swooned when they saw the bodies of their loved-ones. There were 50 chairs set up in the Horticultural Building for mourning. However, the weather was bitterly cold and the building was unheated. Hearses waited outside to take the bodies to the places specified by the family. The cost of transporting was paid by the state. One hundred bodies had been claimed by noon that day. This process

The Rebellion Following the Fire

continued for several days.

Amanda, on behalf of her father, handled telephone inquiries and other matters regarding the victims, including issuing passes for claiming bodies at the fairgrounds. One of the telephone calls she took was from a mother who had heard that her son, Harry, had died, but she had gone to the fairgrounds and had been unable to locate his body. She and Harry had been neighbors of the Thomas family prior to Amanda's dad becoming the warden. "Is Harry dead, Amanda?" the mother asked.

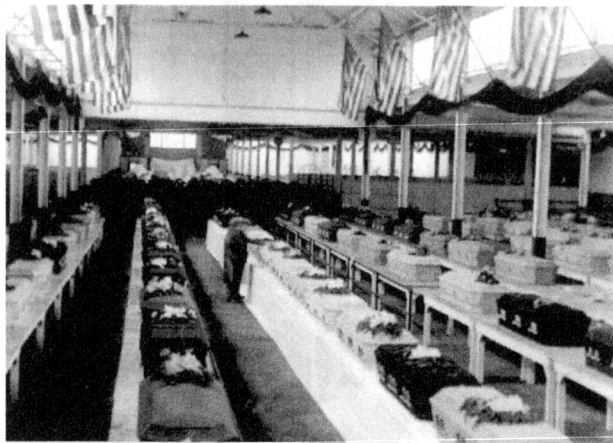

Coffins at the fairgrounds
Courtesy of the Ohio History Connection

Amanda sadly replied, "I'm afraid so, Rose." She then helped her find his body.

As of Wednesday, 133 injured convicts were still in the prison hospital.

On this day, Warden Thomas made his first appearance before the prisoners since the fire when he stepped out of the administrative offices to look around. He stood silently with his head bowed as he listened to Cellblock G&H prisoners, now housed in the chapel, denouncing him. Thomas, who had always prided himself on his fairness and justice to every man within the

The Rebellion Following the Fire

prison walls and the cooperation and discipline he had established with the prisoners, gazed toward the chapel hearing himself jeered and listening to catcalls and oaths directed at him. His eyes were bloodshot from lack of sleep; he struggled to retain his composure. After listening for a minute or two, he said to the priest who was with him, "And after all we have done for them and tried to do," and then turned and went back into the administrative offices.

Notwithstanding the rumor that the prisoners were planning an early-morning attempt to escape, the Board of Inquiry continued its investigation. Upon his arrival at the penitentiary, Attorney General Bettman told reporters on hand that he was determined to learn the facts necessary to get "to the bottom of this tragedy."

Bettman and four others, including the superintendent of construction, E. L. Jenkins, inspected New Hall, but the inspection threw little light on the origin of the blaze. During the inspection, convicts refused to obey the order of Superintendent Jenkins when he attempted to get a group to move out of their way. When he said, "Move on." one of them responded, "Make us move and see what you get." Another prisoner said, "Bring the Warden out here, and we'll tear him to pieces." The superintendent backed off.

Additional National Guard troops were sent to the penitentiary as requested by prison officials because so many hostile prisoners were loose within the prison and in answer to the report that prisoners planned to attempt an escape.

Warden Thomas and a member of the Board of Clemency began

preparing a list of convicts who would be transferred to the London Prison Farm to relieve congestion at the penitentiary.

Thursday, April 24, 1930

Unrest in the prison was at a very high level by Thursday morning. By then the convicts of "White City," had been liberated from their cells for a couple of days and had been milling freely in their cellblocks' corridors. Dissension had spread among them. They sent an ultimatum to the warden demanding the release of the prisoners of "K Company," the "bad boy" company, from their cells. The prisoners of White City threatened that they were prepared to kill guards, if this demand and their other demands weren't met. The guard who delivered the White City ultimatum to the warden trembled in fear with tears streaming down his cheeks as he pleaded with the warden not to send him back to his post. Prison officials gave in to the prisoners' demand and released the prisoners of "K Company" from their cells.

Additional soldiers were mobilized and sent to the prison to augment the prison's defenders.

A priest and two other ministers, well known by the prisoners, went into White City to try to pacify the convicts and plead for order, stressing the suffering and deaths that would result from a riot.

The prisoners asked for a conference with Hal Griswold, the State Director of Welfare, to make their demands known. Griswold said that he would consider written requests. Deputy Warden Woodard went into White City with paper and pencils, and the prisoners wrote down their requests. Warden Thomas learned that one of their requests was for smoking and chewing tobacco, and he ordered that it be furnished forthwith.

Ohio National Guard Colonel Robert Haubrich, commander of the military personnel on duty at the penitentiary, then consisting of National Guard personnel and Naval Reservists, also went into White City and talked to the prisoners' leaders. He reported to Warden Thomas that he believed the prisoners did not intend to become violent, but did intend to carry out passive resistance by refusing to work or obey orders until their demands were met.

A decision by Governor Cooper to delay the execution for 30 days of a prisoner, John Richardson, that was scheduled to take place the next night, Friday, April 25, so that the Ohio Board of Clemency could give careful consideration to an appeal he had made to them, helped to pacify the rebels a little.

That afternoon Attorney General Bettman and Welfare Director Griswold left the meeting of the Board of Inquiry and went to the statehouse to recommend to the governor that he suspend Warden Preston Thomas.

Realizing that the prison regime would not give in to their demands unless forced to do so and understanding that they could not win a fight against the military forces on duty at the prison, the convicts decided upon a campaign of passive resistance and "the pen" to win their demands. The prisoners felt that their relief had to come from the public, and they wanted to take this opportunity to make their case to the people of Ohio. They believed that by refusing to work, refusing to obey orders, and by informing the public of their complaints, the public would be sympathetic to them and support their demands.

To that end, the convicts formed an organization of prisoners which they called the "Committee of Forty for Facts," and announced its formation to reporters. The committee consisted of captains of each range of the cellblocks where the men were then being quartered. The range captains were to hear and pass on to the committee as a whole, for its consideration, the suggestions of inmates in their range. The convicts said that the captains had been picked for their brains, not their brawn.

Members of the Committee of Forty for Facts
Courtesy of the Ohio History Connection

The committee made a set of rules to govern the prisoners to replace the rules of the prison regime. The committee was to enforce the rules. The committee was also to find ways to inform the public of the mistreatment and injustices committed against the prisoners by penitentiary officials.

Following are rules decided upon that were to be enforced by the committee. Prisoners were to:

Look after the welfare of the other prisoners,

Only do work necessary to maintain the well-being of the prisoners, particularly of the injured in the hospital,

Refuse to be locked in cells until they were convinced they would be safe from fire,

Stick together in order to bring about the removal of Warden Thomas,

Suppress radicalism,

Devise no "escape plans,"

Not riot,

Make no demands of their own,

Commit absolutely no violence,

Not participate in any grudge fights, and

Go unshaven.

Concerning their refusal to be locked in cells, the committee's spokesman reminded the reporters present that they had seen their buddies die like rats screaming for help that never came. "Do you blame us for wanting to be sure there won't be a similar disaster befall the other fellows in here? Isn't there exactly the same type of roof over our heads in this block as there was over the burned building?"

The committee's spokesman assured those present that no fair-

The Rebellion Following the Fire

minded guard or just official would be harmed, but warned against letting the warden show his face. "Someone's to blame for the catastrophe, and we blame the warden."

The spokesman said the prisoners had "no chance if Warden Thomas stayed, because he hates all the convicts, except his snitches," but promised that the prisoners would work hard when Thomas was removed.

When asked how long the convicts would continue with this nonviolent plan, the spokesman said, "Well, we will wait till the governor acts, anyway."

The plans of the self-appointed leaders took a blow later that afternoon when Governor Cooper announced that he would not follow the attorney general's recommendation for the removal of Warden Thomas. The governor said that he would "back the warden if it takes every National Guard unit in the state."

Warden Thomas then issued the following statement to the prisoners: "If order is not restored by evening, I will restore it, even if it takes soldiers with drawn bayonets to cover every prisoner."

Dr. Keil reported that there were still 127 prisoners being treated in the prison hospital.

Friday, April 25, 1930

The prisoners seemed to accept the governor's decision and went to breakfast Friday morning in an orderly manner for the first time in four days. Cat calls and hooting were absent, and the guards were amazed at the absence of the shouting, howling mob, refusing to take orders, which the guards had witnessed since Monday. Eight convicts even volunteered to work shoveling coal in the power plant to relieve prisoners who had been at it ever since the fire.

It was announced that the population of the penitentiary would be reduced by over four hundred by May 1, because the Ohio Board of Clemency had advanced the dates for paroling some prisoners and because other prisoners would be transferred to the Mansfield Reformatory and the London Prison Farm.

Convicts marching to breakfast in an orderly fashion
Courtesy of the Ohio History Connection

It was also announced that John Hall had been replaced by Frank Laukhart as night captain of the guards.

[NOTE: This was the result of a voluntary, self-imposed, suspension by Captain Hall.]

Saturday, April 26, 1930

On this day, 40 unclaimed victims of the fire were buried in three Columbus cemeteries, East Lawn, Mt. Calvary, and Evergreen. The funeral procession was escorted by the 13th Battalion, Naval Reserve, of Columbus. Shortly after 2:00 p.m. last rites were given over the bodies. About 2,000 people attended the event. Each grave was marked by a metal disc bearing the prisoner's accounting number that appears on the prison records, thereby making it possible for persons to claim the remains in the future.

Naval Reservists preparing for burial of unclaimed bodies
Courtesy of the Ohio History Connection

The Columbus Chamber of Commerce and Franklin Lodge No. 5, Knights of Pythias passed resolutions commending Governor Cooper for his handling of the penitentiary fire and investigation, and in particular, in refusing to act in accordance with the demands of the prisoners and others for the removal of Warden Thomas.

Although things seemed to have settled down in the prison, there were signs that many of the prisoners had not been pacified.

The Rebellion Following the Fire

Prisoners continued their passive resistance, refusing to go to work and refusing to permit employees of the prison to repair jammed locks and wrecked cells.

On Saturday night, in order to provide quick communication in the event of further trouble, National Guardsmen completed the installation of a field telephone system that connected every tower on the prison wall to the Ohio National Guard headquarters, which had been established on Spring St., across the street from the penitentiary.

Sunday, April 27, 1930

On Sunday, April 27, memorial services were held for the fire victims at the prison's Catholic chapel, Protestant chapel, and Jewish synagogue.

There was much public anxiety over what might happen at the centrally located prison and in the city, if there was a breakout as many feared. In the minds of the residents, the situation at the penitentiary had gone back and forth several times following the fire between "things are getting better" to "things are getting worse." On Sunday, many people drove or walked to the penitentiary to get a glimpse of the Columbus policemen, the National Guard, and the Naval Reserve troops, who were protecting them.

Later in the day, convicts heard that additional guards were to be put on duty on Monday to end the "passive resistance" campaign against Warden Thomas. An uprising resulted during which cell doors in White City were torn off. Eventually, the uprising was quelled by persuasion and by furnishing the convicts with a large quantity of coffee. During the uprising a Bible taken from one of the convicts was found to contain a knife and several saw blades, and it was reported that other prisoners had possession of large pieces of iron and other objects that could be used as weapons.

During the day and into the evening, Warden Thomas held a meeting in the administrative offices with Colonel Haubrich, Columbus Chief of Police, Harry French, Deputy Warden Woodard, Captain H. E. Laukart (the new night captain), and William Duffy, Columbus Service Director. At the meeting, Warden Thomas stated to those in attendance that the time had come to clamp down on the prisoners. He was assured by those at the meeting that any steps he took would be backed up by them. Captain Laukhart reported that he had made trips through the prison and declared that as a whole, the convicts, other than those in "White City," were quieter than they had been since the fire. Although the time to begin clamping down was not announced to the public, all indications were that it would be the next day.

An allotment of maces was delivered to the warden for use in the event of a serious uprising. Warden Thomas was seen putting two pistols in his pocket as he was climbing the stairs to his quarters after the meeting.

The warden's daughter, Amanda, assisted her father in his office during the day and evening, with a wicked looking "six shooter" in her right hand or within easy reach. Amanda made it a practice to always have a gun with her.

The Rebellion Following the Fire

Monday, April 28, 1930

The warden's order for the day was to "quell the rebellion and return order and discipline to the penitentiary." The Columbus Police Department contributed 150 armed policemen to the effort under the command of Chief Harry French. All of these men were deployed inside the penitentiary early Monday morning in accordance with plans made on Sunday.

National Guardsmen prepared for action
Courtesy of the Ohio History Connection

The National Guard contributed 350 armed soldiers under the command of Colonel Haubrich. They were on hand outside the walls to be used if needed. Colonel Haubrich said that the number of troops could be increased to 1,200 in a very short time, if necessary. Several machine guns were mounted at strategic locations.

Two hundred prison guards, including 35 new guards, marched the convicts to breakfast from the various cellblocks and dormitories as police stood by armed with rifles, shotguns, pistols, night sticks, and teargas bombs. The police were told to shoot to kill if active resistance developed, but the prisoners did not resist.

The Rebellion Following the Fire

Prisoners waiting to be taken to the London Prison Farm
Courtesy of the Columbus Dispatch

Also during the morning hours, 52 of what were thought to be the leaders of the rebellious White City convicts were removed and sent to the London Prison Farm. The hope was that doing so would help to end the rebellion.

However, at lunchtime, when it was their turn to go to the dining hall, the White City prisoners sent word out that they would not leave White City to go to lunch until all policemen were removed from within the walls. They yelled that they, "couldn't trust police on the outside and wouldn't trust them here." They claimed they had stored a 60-day supply of food in their cells, and they had weapons. Warden Thomas had the police leave. As the police marched east on Spring Street past White City's windows, the prisoners booed and cursed them and called them names. Even after the police were removed, the convicts refused to leave White City and said if prison officials wanted them to eat they could bring the food to them. Warden Thomas and Colonel Haubrich conferred as a squad of 12 guards equipped with gas masks and tear gas bombs awaited orders in the prison yard. The warden's answer was, "They will stay right in there, and they will starve until they are ready to come out and obey orders." He announced that the prisoners would get "no more concessions."

The Rebellion Following the Fire

Father O'Brien visited White City and reported that it appeared to him the prison officials had only succeeded in removing the "talkers" to London and that the real leaders of the revolt were still at work inciting the other convicts.

Next, Deputy Warden Woodard went into White City and tried to persuade them to cooperate. At first, they told him that he had "double-crossed them" and rejected his plea to submit to authority. The convicts said they would adhere to their plan of resistance "until hell froze over." Eventually, Woodard convinced them to go out and promised them they would not be harmed. At 12:50 p.m., the prisoners marched to lunch, except for one prisoner who stayed behind.

Governor Cooper issued a statement making it clear that he fully supported Warden Thomas's efforts to restore order at the penitentiary.

A chest containing chisels, hatchets, and other tools, which could be used as weapons was found by guards in the afternoon in the chapel building.

White City was peaceful during the afternoon, but the peace was short lived. At 6:00 p.m., the prisoners in White City started a demonstration and disabled the lights, putting the entire cell house into darkness.

To remedy that situation, firemen cut holes in the roof over White City, and flood lights were lowered through the holes and suspended above the cellblocks.

Colonel Haubrich and several guardsmen entered the prison and made an inspection of a tunnel connecting the power plant to various parts of the prison, including White City. It was feared that the convicts had gained access to the tunnel and that they might have plans to disable the power plant, thereby shutting off the electricity in the penitentiary.

Firemen cutting holes in the roof of White City for lights
Courtesy of the Columbus Dispatch

Colonel Haubrich and his party spent about an hour searching the tunnel but found no convicts in the tunnel and no evidence that they had been there. Nonetheless, arrangements were made to connect the penitentiary to the city's power plant to provide power to the prison in the event the prison's power plant was shut down.

That night there were nearly 1,000 National Guard troops assigned to night duty at the prison.

During the night, an automobile near the prison backfired several times. The convicts in White City, thinking they were revolver shots, yelled, cursed, and smashed windows. Police Chief Harry

The Rebellion Following the Fire

French was apprised of the situation and troops at Fort Hayes were advised to hold themselves in readiness. The public was barred from the streets and sidewalks within two blocks of the prison. Automobile traffic was detoured.

The situation settled down around midnight. The prisoners sent a request for decks of playing cards, which was granted. During the night, many of the convicts gambled with dice and cards for tobacco, clothing and money.

The prisoners were in control inside the walls. They even had access to the commissary and could take anything they wanted. The prisoners' leaders charged a fee to prisoners for access to the commissary. That night 800 pork chops were stolen and cooked by convicts over fires made in White City using magazines and other materials. There was no one to stop them. Guards could do nothing to control the prisoners. They were outnumbered about fifty to one, and to make matters worse, the guards were unarmed, and many of the prisoners carried items that could be used as weapons. The prison administration did not allow guards to carry weapons when they were within reach of the convicts for fear the convicts would seize the weapons. Therefore, the guards had to do their jobs unarmed, knowing that some convicts were armed and harbored hatred toward them.

The guards were insulted and menaced by the inmates. Many of them fled their posts. By daybreak on Tuesday, just five guards remained on duty in White City, and their only real function was to spy on the prisoners and report their activities.

Tuesday, April 29, 1930 - Riot

The Rebellion Following the Fire

Making the repairs to White City necessitated moving the convicts out while the repairs were being made. Various strategies were put forth to deal with that problem. One made by Colonel Haubrich was that all 1,300 prisoners in White City be transferred to city and county jails throughout the state or that a stockade be built at the fairgrounds and the prisoners transferred there. The move to temporary prisons would thwart any escape preparations then underway and would enable repairs to be made so that order could be restored in White City.

Colonel Haubrich's idea was rejected because of the logistics that would have been involved and the increased possibility of escape. Instead, prison officials decided to construct a fenced stockade on the prison baseball field and house the prisoners from White City in tents within the stockade.

Colonel Haubrich
Courtesy of the Columbus Dispatch

Regardless of where the prisoners would be housed while the repairs were made, they would first have to be removed from White City. The prisoners, who had been roaming free within the building for a week, showed no signs that they would be cooperative, but the officials decided that the holes cut in the roof by the firemen for the lights could be used to "flush" the convicts out with water or teargas.

When the White City convicts realized what was being planned,

The Rebellion Following the Fire

they rioted. A total of 1,300 prisoners took part in the riot. The prisoners, armed with iron bars and other offensive weapons they had fashioned swarmed to the entrance to the guardroom, located on the west side of White City. Six guards and three National Guardsmen were in the guardroom. The prison guards and National Guardsmen positioned themselves strategically in the room with their guns. The prisoners bombarded the partition separating the guardroom from White City with bolts, rocks and other small missiles picked up in the yard. Unable to break into the guardroom they backed off, but then made a second assault. The door bulged and a glass panel in the door broke, but the iron bars on the door kept the prisoners out. When the second rush was made shots were fired from within the guardroom, but no one was hit. The prisoners scattered but regrouped and made a third attempt to break down the door. Once again, shots were fired. This time two convicts were hit, one in the groin and the other in the leg.

The prisoners then retreated, taking two guards with them as hostages. One of the guards taken hostage was hit in the head with a stool during the melee. The prisoners threatened to kill the guards, but later voluntarily released them, and the situation quieted. The prisoners who had been shot were taken to the prison hospital. The prisoner who was shot through the groin was in serious condition.

When the governor was made aware of what was going on, he turned control of the penitentiary over to Colonel Haubrich and his troops, with instructions to "take all necessary steps to disarm the prisoners and quell the mutiny." Colonel Haubrich ordered the

The Rebellion Following the Fire

guards out of the prison yard and established his headquarters in the prison's chapel. He posted 150 of his men at strategic positions inside the prison. Guardsmen leveled their rifles at the windows of White City where the prisoners were yelling and cursing. Next, he and members of his staff went to White City and talked to the prisoners, telling them that further resistance was useless and assuring them there would be no more shooting if they behaved. The prisoners agreed to behave.

The riot began around 10:00 a.m. and ended at around 11:00 a.m. During the one-hour riot, several small fires were started by prisoners, and it was rumored that convicts had access to several hundred gallons of gasoline. Because of the threat of further rioting and fires, the records of the criminal identification bureau, which were normally stored at the penitentiary, were removed from the offices to a location across the street from the prison.

At noon, shouts of derision greeted prison guards when they entered White City to escort the hard-boiled convict contingent to their meal, but the harassment was checked by the prompt appearance of soldiers carrying rifles. Escorted by prison guards and flanked by guardsmen with loaded rifles and fixed bayonets, the prisoners marched to the mess hall silently but with furtive glances at the military men and also at nests of machine guns mounted on buildings. At 12:40 p.m., the last of the White City occupants left the building.

Eight more of the leaders of the rebellion were put in solitary confinement. Several prisoners asked to be separated from the White City prisoners for their protection from the rebels.

Work began on building a stockade in the prison yard, using barbed-wire fences. Army tents measuring 15' by 15' were set up in the stockade.

[NOTE: When completed, there were 88 tents and each housed up to ten convicts. The stockade's total capacity was 880 convicts. The most unruly prisoners from White City were moved to the stockade when it was ready for occupancy the next day.]

During the riot on Tuesday, four of the seven men on death row were liberated by White City rebels who battered down the death house cell doors. The other three chose to remain in their cells. The liberated death row inmates changed from street clothes (normally worn by death row inmates) into prison garb and roamed around with the other prisoners.

George Williams, age 68, and Charles Hanovich, age 20, had been partners in a crime which resulted in the death of a Cleveland police officer. Williams shot the cop, and Hanovich turned

White city inmates show off damage done to their cellblock -- Third from the left (holding a pipe) is Charles Hanovich
Courtesy of the Columbus Dispatch

state's evidence against Williams and received a life sentence, which he was serving at the penitentiary. Williams was sentenced to death in the electric chair on the strength of Hanovich's testimony and was scheduled to die on June 28. Williams was one of the death row inmates liberated during the riot. When Williams was liberated in the morning by the rebellious convicts, he set out on a hunt for Hanovich, intending to kill his former partner. Williams told other convicts, "I can't be penalized any more for taking another life." Hanovich got word that Williams was on the loose and looking for him. He hid. Williams had murdered four people during his 40-year criminal career, and Hanovich knew Williams would kill him if he had a chance. Williams didn't find him. As he was leaving the mess hall after supper, Williams was spotted by guards and locked up again.

Although Williams never got to Hanovich, Hanovich was beaten that night in White City with a piece of pipe by a prisoner of the "tougher element" because he had testified against his partner. Hanovich was hospitalized, but survived the beating.

Death row inmates being transferred to the city jail
Courtesy of the Columbus Dispatch

After this incident, all the death row inmates were transferred to the Columbus City Prison. At the city prison one of the condemned told of a plot by some of the other death row inmates to kill their guard and make a break for freedom. They felt that since they were going to die anyhow, they might just as well be shot in an attempted escape as to be electrocuted.

[NOTE: The condemned men complained about the food at the city jail saying that prisoners on death row at the penitentiary received better food.]

Another convict was badly beaten with a pipe in White City Tuesday night. He was a trusty and was accused of "playing in with prison officials." He was also taken to the prison hospital.

The number of fire victims still in the prison hospital was now 99.

Wednesday, April 30, 1930

The trouble-making convicts of White City were sullen on Wednesday, but there was a lack of rebellious activity on their part.

After gaining control of the prison, the National Guard rushed to complete the 11-foot-high barbed-wire stockade on the prison baseball field and to set up tents to house the White City gang.

The National Guardsmen and Naval Reservists made the convicts "toe the mark." The convicts respected them, their rifles, and the machine guns which were manned and pointed at them. However, they continued deriding and harassing the prison guards, unless military personnel intervened.

Some of the non-rebellious prisoners housed in White City persisted in begging guards to separate them from the troublemakers. Since they were not participating in the rebellion, they feared that they might be beaten like the two prisoners beaten on Tuesday night. On that night, non-rebellious convicts had grouped together for protection and took turns sleeping, leaving someone awake to guard the others from attack by troublemakers. They told guards that they were willing to sleep on the ground if they were just separated from "the red shirt gang." In order to give some security to the non-rebellious prisoners, five-hundred of the most unruly prisoners from White City were housed that night in the penitentiary's auto tag warehouse, away from the others.

A telegram saying only "ON TO COLUMBUS!" was received at the National Guard headquarters at the prison that day, the day before "May Day." It was sent from Cleveland and was signed, "The Committee." Many "May Day" gatherings celebrating communism were scheduled to take place around the country on Thursday, May 1, 1930, by communistic organizations. It was suspected that the telegram had been sent by such an organization and that they intended to cause further trouble at the prison.

Officials of Allen County informed the governor that they were willing to assume responsibility and temporary care of the 28 prisoners from that county who were confined in the penitentiary. The offer was made for the purposes of helping to relieve congestion at the prison and to protect the prisoners from Allen County from the danger of riots.

It was reported that in order to relieve congestion during the crisis at the penitentiary, a total of 600 convicts had been transferred to the London Prison Farm. That facility was designed for a maximum capacity of 500 inmates. At the time of the penitentiary fire, it was already very over-crowded with a total population of 1,000. Now, with the additional 600 from the penitentiary, its population was 1,600.

Acting on a report that some letters addressed to convicts had been found to contain saw blades, prison officials ordered all incoming mail to be examined.

While convicts from G&H Cellblock ate their lunch, their quarters in the prison chapel were searched, and various weapons were found in their beds, including butcher knives, cleavers, hammers, hatchets, and wire cutters.

The Stockade
Courtesy of the Columbus Dispatch

At 6:00 p.m. prisoners housed in White City were marched to their temporary quarters in the newly completed stockade as guardsmen stood by with rifles and fixed bayonets. The prisoners were to be housed there until the damages in the cellblocks were repaired and fireproof roofs were placed over the cellblocks.

Weapons, including knives, makeshift daggers, and saws were confiscated from the prisoners as they were marched into the stockade. Other weapons were found along the sidewalk leading to the stockade, dropped there by prisoners knowing that they would be searched.

Machine guns looked down from prison walls and from roofs of buildings. The troops on the ground were armed with rifles and pistols. Hand grenades were within easy reach. Hence, even the most hard-boiled prisoners followed the orders of military troops.

National Guardsmen with machine gun
Courtesy of the Columbus Dispatch

The stockade was reminiscent of the Confederate Prison at Andersonville during the Civil War, in that there were orders to the men guarding the prisoners to shoot to kill any prisoner who crossed its deadline.

Thursday, May 1, 1930

Prison officials believed that the prisoners in White City had been attempting to dig a tunnel for an escape and that the prisoners' reluctance to leave the cellblock for lunch on Monday was to prevent guards from discovering their work in digging. It was believed that the prisoner who had stayed behind was to keep an eye on the guards and report to the rest of the prisoners on what, if anything, the guards discovered while the rest were at lunch.

An inspection was made of White City, which revealed that 484 cells in A&B and C&D Cellblocks were absolutely useless as a result of the damage done by the rebellious prisoners.

Their inspection also revealed that the prisoners had dug holes through the rear of several cells, into an area between the parallel ranges of cells. That area contained the plumbing pipes for the cellblock. Perhaps escape from the roof, by climbing the piping in the space behind the ranges of cells, was in the prisoners' minds. However, it would have been "curtains" for any prisoner whose head appeared above the cellblock. The roof was guarded by machine guns ready for such an attempt.

Damage in White City
Courtesy of the Columbus Dispatch

Holes in a steel wall big enough to crawl through had been made, and they had also dug their way into the basement under the cell block, and a tunnel had been dug all the way to the outer wall.

The Rebellion Following the Fire

Had the tunnel been completed by going through, or under, the foundation and coming to the surface on the other side, it would have provided an escape route to the lawn between the south prison wall and Spring Street.

Besides digging, the convicts had made a failed attempt to batter down the iron-barred windows connecting their cellblock with the "honor dormitory" at the southeast corner of the prison. Had they gained access to the "honor dormitory" only a large wooden door would have barred their path to the outside. However, a manned machine gun was trained on that door, over which hung a bright light. Eleven other machine guns had been placed at strategic points around the prison.

After the inspection, cells were cleared of personal belongings. One prisoner from each cell was brought in from the stockade to pack the bedding and personal effects of all convicts quartered in his cell.

Military personnel then escorted newspaper reporters and photographers through the cellblocks, so they could see the destruction first hand. The cellblocks were unoccupied at that time except by a lonely cat, apparently the White City mascot. Not a lock was intact on any of the cells; all 800 had been destroyed. They had been jimmied, plugged with matches, or battered off. Scores of cell doors had been ripped off, and the latches and bolts of others had been bent and twisted so that the doors could not be locked. Doors that had been torn off were stacked at the end of the ranges.

The reporters were also shown the death row "annex," which had

The Rebellion Following the Fire

been totally destroyed by convicts sympathetic with the plight of the condemned.

After the reporters' tour was over, repairmen surveyed the work to be done.

On Thursday, the governor received a petition signed by 900 residents of Newark, Zanesville, and Mansfield commending him for his handling of the penitentiary fire situation and the subsequent revolt of convicts and imploring him to retain Thomas as the warden of the penitentiary. The petition congratulated him for his courage in refusing to comply with the demands of the revolting convicts that Thomas be removed.

Colonel Haubrich heeded the warning "On to Columbus!" contained in Wednesday's telegram from Cleveland and took precautions against a possible "May Day" demonstration, but the warning turned out to be a false alarm. The "Committee" didn't show up.

Late Thursday night a cab driver drove into the zone near the prison that was off limits and failed to stop when ordered. Four different National Guardsmen fired at the cab as it sped away. The 23-year-old cab driver was tracked down using the cab's identification number and arrested the next day.

Friday, May 2, 1930

The regular prison guards in their blue uniforms and brass buttons were present at the penitentiary, but the National Guardsmen dressed in khaki were the ones in control. The prison grounds resounded to the marching of military troops with rifles on their

The Rebellion Following the Fire

shoulders. The prison guards continued to patrol without weapons, protected by the guardsmen. The convicts were orderly, realizing that tear gas bombs and hand grenades were within easy reach of the soldiers and that from the prison walls and other strategic points, machine guns were pointed at them.

Warden Thomas, in his office in the administration building, continued to arrange for the transfer of prisoners to various other jails to relieve congestion. He also requested county officials throughout the state to hold their prisoners in their respective county jails until conditions at the penitentiary were back to normal.

The warden's efficient daughter, Amanda, with her snub-nosed revolver, was constantly at her father's side, helping him in every way she could.

By then, the tension that had hung over the penitentiary since the fire had mostly lifted. Prisoners were gradually returning to work, and repairs were being made in White City. Locksmiths were repairing the locks; doors torn from the cells were being replaced. Some of the forty or more out-of-town newspaper men who had gone to Columbus to report on the fire had returned home. Others were spending their time playing cards. The order that the public was not permitted in certain areas near the penitentiary had been revoked.

The prison hospital reported that the number of convicts still being treated at the hospital was down to 70, and all were expected to recover.

The Rebellion Following the Fire

"The war is over!" declared Colonel Haubrich, the World War veteran who commanded the 1,000 National Guardsmen and Naval Reservists on duty at the penitentiary, the largest armed military force assembled in Ohio since the World War.

The report of the Board of Inquiry was delivered to the governor.

On the lighter side: During the cleanup of White City a radio was found in a wrecked cell that, upon examination, was found not to be a radio at all. Inside was a "still" containing nearly two gallons of an alcoholic liquid described by some as being like peach brandy. Also inside the radio cabinet, there were bottles, corks, copper tubing, copper dippers, and a complete kit of repair tools. Officials speculated that the prisoners who operated the still probably got their raw materials from the prison's pantry in the form of canned fruits. It was assumed that the finished product was peddled to fellow prisoners in White City, which would help to explain the courage displayed by them during the rebellion.

Saturday, May 3, 1930

Charles Hanovich, who had testified against his partner in crime, George Williams, and who was beaten by another prisoner with a piece of pipe on Tuesday night for having done so, was transferred from the hospital to the London Prison Farm for his protection.

White City prisoners continued to harass guards in whatever way they could. Many of the "bad boys" removed the identification numbers on their uniforms and gave false names when asked to identify themselves.

The Rebellion Following the Fire

During the turmoil at the time of the Easter Monday fire one young prisoner, Mike Dorn, escaped. He was a barber and was at the prison hospital cutting hair when the fire started. He helped take care of the injured inmates through the night. Shortly before dawn on the morning after the fire, he put on a hat and a doctor's white coat, slung a stethoscope around his neck, and picked up a medical case. He walked across the prison yard and through the main gate, unchallenged. Two doctors gave him a ride downtown. From there he went by bus to Toledo where friends provided him with a change of clothes. Then he and his girlfriend went on a two-week vacation, traveling in Ohio, Pennsylvania, New York, and New Jersey and ending in Cleveland. He was captured in Cleveland at a rooming house after the Cleveland police received a tip as to his whereabouts from an anonymous female caller. Perhaps his girlfriend was afraid that if she continued to hang out with him she might end up in prison herself. Dorn said he was getting pretty tired of being on the "dodge" anyway. He was returned to the penitentiary on May 3. Warden Thomas didn't punish Dorn. He said he was a good prisoner and laughed it off as being just a matter of "young love" and the "call of spring."

Mike Dorn
Courtesy of the Ohio History Connection

Sunday, May 4, 1930

On Sunday night, a prisoner was found badly beaten and nearly dead on his cot in the stockade. There were several deep cuts on his head, and he had lost a lot of blood. It was estimated that he had been on his cot bleeding for two hours before the guards found him. Guards were told that he had been beaten by two prisoners in retaliation for him squealing on them more than three years earlier concerning some infraction of rules at the penitentiary. Retaliation was delayed because he escaped from the penitentiary in April 1927 and was only recently returned. He was taken to the prison hospital. The beating was so severe and the loss of blood was so great that hospital personnel did not expect him to live. The attackers' identities were not known by authorities, and the inmates refused to squeal on them.

The Stockade
Courtesy of the Ohio History Connection

Another prisoner was beaten on Sunday night in E&F dormitory.

The motive for that beating was never known, and once again, no one was willing to tell who the attacker was.

A prisoner being locked in a cell is not all bad. Almost anyone who might have a grudge against him is locked out. The prisoner only has his cellmates to worry about.

Monday, May 5, 1930

Three prison shops were reopened on Monday: the auto tag factory, the tin shop, and the printing plant.

Warden Thomas received a letter from another organization (this time it was from the "Committee on Human Rights" of Portland, Oregon) blaming him for the death of the 320 convicts killed in the fire and threatening vengeance against him.

Tuesday, May 6, 1930

By May 6, all shops at the Penitentiary were in operation, except the cotton and woolen mills, which would not be reopened until conditions returned to normal because those shops contained expensive equipment that might have been damaged or destroyed if there was further trouble.

Prison officials continued their efforts to separate disorderly prisoners from those who were cooperative, and additional plans were made to transfer unmanageable prisoners to other prisons.

Hospital personnel reported that the prisoner who had been beaten in the stockade Sunday night was improving and was now expected to live. It took 63 stitches to close his cuts.

It was also reported that the prisoner who was shot in the groin during the April 29 riot had been transferred to White Cross Hospital for surgery, but was expected to live.

Trouble in identifying prisoners continued. Twenty-five prisoners were put in chained cells in White City and put on a bread and water diet for refusing to identify themselves.

Thursday, May 8, 1930 – More Loss of Life

Colonel Haubrich learned that the war was not completely over.

Shortly after midnight on the morning of Thursday, May 8, the tents in the stockade were set on fire by the convicts being housed there. A prisoner passed from tent to tent firing them with burning paper. Prisoners then pushed other tents into the burning tents to set them on fire. Many convicts gleefully watched the tents burn. Convicts were given buckets of water to use to fight the fires, but did little effective work with them.

Tents burned by the prisoners
Courtesy of the Ohio History Connection

All the tents were destroyed except one. Not all

The Rebellion Following the Fire

prisoners even undertook to save their cots and bed clothing. Colonel Haubrich announced that it would be impossible to provide other shelter by nightfall and that the convicts would have to be exposed to the elements until other shelter could be provided. The prisoners' laughter died out as the fact that they had destroyed their only shelter sunk in. On that day, the temperature rose to 86 degrees. As the day wore on, some convicts constructed shelter from the sun using tent poles and partially burned tent material.

Colonel Haubrich, responding to the threat that the burning of the tents might lead to more rebellious activity, doubled the number of National Guardsmen on duty in the area of the stockade, and had additional machine guns mounted.

Shortly after 6:00 a.m. a further tragedy occurred at the prison. Bullets were accidentally discharged from a machine gun, which had been mounted in front of the prison chapel after the fire in the stockade. The accidental discharge occurred when the National Guardsman manning the gun was loading a belt of ammunition. Two convicts were killed, and another injured by the bullets. Those killed were asleep at the time in the E&F Dormitory. One of those killed had spent two days being treated at the prison hospital for burns he received while carrying fire victims of the April 21 fire out of the G&H Cellblock after he was released from his cell in White City.

The stockade prisoners were punished for setting the tents on fire and for not making a genuine effort to put them out by not being given their morning and noon meals. In the evening they were offered bread and water, but they refused to eat and declared a hunger strike.

Guard Thomas Watkinson was back on the job after a 17-day suspension.

Friday, May 9, 1930

The stockade residents were again offered bread and water in the morning and at noon, which they again refused. However, when it was time for the afternoon meal, they gave in to their hunger and ate the bread tossed into the stockade, ending their short-lived hunger strike. They were removed from the stockade on Friday evening. Some of the prisoners were sent to Cellblock A in White City, some to dormitories E&F and the rest to various other buildings.

On the positive side, eighty percent of the prisoners who had been housed in the stockade were now asking for work.

As a result of the transfer of some prisoners to other facilities and the early parole of others, the penitentiary population was about 1,200 less than at the time of the fire.

By now G&H Cellblock had been cleaned up and was ready for repairs to be made, and a fireproof roof over E&F Dormitory was under construction.

Saturday, May 10, 1930

Prison officials reported that the convicts were being cooperative and following orders, the rebels had been completely segregated from the rest of the prisoners, and the conditions inside the penitentiary were nearer normalcy than at any time since the fire.

However, guards instituted a search of the stockade on this day, following rumors that three or four of the prisoners housed in the stockade had been murdered and buried beneath the debris of burned tents.

[NOTE: There was no further mention of this matter in news reports, and therefore it appears to have been a false rumor.]

Wednesday, May 14, 1930

Several guards complained that soap had been put in the soup they were served at lunch.

Thursday, May 15, 1930

Reporters had not been allowed inside the penitentiary since control was given to the National Guard on April 29, but today were allowed to make a detailed inspection and found that the prison was now functioning much as it had prior to the fire.

They also learned that the stockade, which had been built to temporarily house White City convicts, was being converted into a camp for the treatment and housing of convicts with tuberculosis.

Following are other things they learned during their inspection:

An investigation of the behavior of the prisoners during the insurgency had led officials to classify 10% of the prisoners as the "leaders of the rebellion, 25% as followers, and the other 65% as having neither the initiative nor the desire to join either of the groups. The investigation also showed that ninety percent of the rebellion's leaders were serving long-term sentences;

The Columbus Board of Health reviewed the death certificates of the 320 convicts who died in the fire and found that 134 of them were less than 30 years old, 122 were between 30 and 40, and 64 were over 40;

The Board of Health reported that since the military took control of the prison, the number of baths received by the convicts had increased from one per week to two per week, and after each bath the prisoners were given clean garments;

650 National Guardsmen were working inside the walls and none were patrolling outside the walls; and

Warden Thomas had resumed his routine duties at the prison.

They also received a report that the warden had made the following rule changes:

Henceforth, a "double guard" would be stationed around the outside of the prison.

The long-standing practice of allowing visitors to inspect the penitentiary would be stopped.

Convicts out-going mail would be censored and letters reflecting their attitudes would be put in their files for consideration by the clemency board at parole hearings.

Wednesday, May 21, 1930

Warden Thomas announced additional measures to prevent prison breaks. He said that he was acquiring six Thompson sub-machine guns, seven tear gas guns, and six repeating shotguns, and he would be instructing a special squadron in the use of submachine guns and tear gas guns.

Harry Laukhart was appointed captain of the night guards by Warden Thomas, replacing John Hall. Laukhart had been serving as interim night captain since the day after the fire when Hall left that position because he had suffered a breakdown as a result of the strain of the fire tragedy. Laukhart had been the assistant night captain for about a year prior to the fire. Guard Harold Whetstone was appointed to be the new assistant night captain.

Monday, May 26, 1930

John Richardson was executed on this day. His electrocution was originally scheduled for April 25, four days after the fire, but Governor Cooper had delayed it. Richardson's was the first execution since the fire.

Tuesday, May 27, 1930

The last of the National Guardsmen left the penitentiary and control was given back to Warden Thomas. The warden stated that during the transition back to his control and for an indefinite period afterward, the prisoners would not be allowed to

Colonel Haubrich returning control of the penitentiary to Warden Thomas
Courtesy of the Columbus Dispatch

The Rebellion Following the Fire

receive packages and would not be allowed to have visitors.

During the turmoil at the penitentiary members of the Regular Army, the National Guard, and the Naval Reserve had been used to assist penitentiary guards in dealing with the problems. When the governor turned control of the penitentiary over to the National Guard, as many as 1,200 guardsmen were used to maintain order. The National Guard was in control of the penitentiary for 29 days.

Saturday, June 28, 1930

George Williams, the Cleveland man who shot and killed a Cleveland policeman and who tried to find and kill his partner in crime during the riot, was executed.

This murderer of at least four people who had gained the reputation of one of the hardest criminals to face the electric chair was defiant to the end. He refused to give any last statement and told the prison chaplain that he was wasting his time when the chaplain offered him solace. When asked to pray, he refused. His only request was to be permitted to walk to the chair unassisted. When seated in the chair he complained to a guard adjusting a strap around his leg, "You don't have to push it through my leg, do you?" He ate very little of his "last meal," consisting of fried chicken and various side dishes, prepared for him by Mrs. P. E. Thomas, the warden's wife. When it was brought to him, he cursed the guards for bringing it so late (it was near midnight) and said he wasn't hungry because he had eaten at the city jail.

[NOTE: Mrs. Thomas always fixed the last meal for a prisoner who was to be executed and included treats requested by him.]

Thursday, July 31, 1930

Forty "red shirts" were returned to the penitentiary from the Mansfield Reformatory.

This was the last news concerning conditions and problems brought about by the fire and rebellion at the penitentiary.

The prison was crowded prior to the fire, and because of the damage to G&H Cellblock and the loss of the roof over it, along with the vandalism and destruction in White City, the number the prison could house was far less following the fire. The possibility of riot and mass escape presented another reason to lower the prison population. Penitentiary officials and the Ohio Department of Welfare did what they could to reduce it. Many prisoners were transferred to other penal institutions in the state during the revolt, including a large portion of the "bad boy" population. Also, paroles were granted sooner than usual. During the two months following the fire, the prisoner population at the penitentiary dropped from 4,200 to 3,000. Now the prisoners were returning.

Eventually the repairs and improvements, including the fireproof roofs, were completed, and the remaining "red shirts" and other prisoners who had been moved during the turmoil were returned.

Tuesday, September 23, 1930

There was, however, an occurrence at the penitentiary on September 23, 1930, which made the papers. A guard accidentally discharged a shotgun in the warden's office while removing it from a gun rack. At the moment it fired, the gun was pointed at a painting of a pair of adult lions and four cubs hanging on the warden's office wall. Yes, the lions got shot. The painting was one of the warden's favorites and had been painted by a former convict. The warden was out of town at the time of the incident. There was no follow-up report on what he had to say to his "big-game hunting" guard when he returned.

Friday, December 24, 1930

Tacks Latimer, former major league baseball player, leaving the penitentiary after being pardoned by the governor
Courtesy of the Columbus

One of the prisoners at the time of the fire was Clifford "Tacks" Latimer, a former professional baseball player, who played catcher for the Cincinnati Reds and the Pittsburgh Pirates (where he was a teammate of Hall of Famer, Honus Wagner).

After leaving professional baseball, he became a railroad detective for the Pennsylvania Railroad, working in Xenia, Ohio. For some reason, his boss, Charles Mackrodt, was demoted from his position as supervisor of the company's railroad detectives, and he blamed Latimer for his demotion. On November 26, 1924, on the streets of Xenia, Mackrodt, who had previously made threats on Latimer's life, and who

The Rebellion Following the Fire

was known to carry a gun, confronted him. It was payday, and both were in town to pick up their checks. Mackrodt arrived at the railroad office early so he would be sure to meet up with Latimer. During the confrontation Mackrodt accused Latimer of slandering him, brandished a knife, and said, "I'll get you before sundown, if I have to get you in your backyard." Then Latimer saw his boss's hand going into his pocket and believed Mackrodt was drawing his gun. Latimer shot him to death. He was tried for murder. He claimed self-defense and was backed up in that contention by several people. Notwithstanding, the jury found him guilty of second-degree murder. They didn't buy Latimer's explanation that his first shot had turned Mackrodt around, and that was why the shot that killed him hit him in the back. The judge sentenced him to life in prison.

He was sent to the penitentiary where he was a model prisoner. He managed the prison's baseball team and became a trusty, working for Warden Thomas in the administrative offices.

He was a hero during a prison break that took place at the penitentiary on November 8, 1926, when he shielded the warden's daughter, Amanda, from the 13 convicts who made the break through the bullpen and the administrative offices and out the door to Spring Street. He also participated in the pursuit of the escapees and their return to the prison.

On the night of the deadly Easter Monday fire, Amanda issued Latimer a shotgun and posted him to stand guard in the administrative offices.

On Christmas Eve of 1930, Governor Cooper went to the

The Rebellion Following the Fire

penitentiary and personally presented Latimer with a pardon. Before handing Latimer his pardon the governor asked Tacks to tell his story. After Tacks had told the governor how he came to be in the penitentiary, Warden Thomas told the governor about the 1926 prison break and Latimer's part in it. He also told him about Tacks' role on the night of the deadly fire and concluded by saying he thought Tacks should be freed. The governor then turned to Tacks, handed him his pardon, and said, "You're a free man. The pardon came as a surprise to Latimer. Tacks replied, "I want to do the right thing. I want to go home and make a home for my mother and children and grandchildren. You'll never regret what you've done."

[NOTE: The November 8, 1926, prison break and the capture of the escapees could not have been more dramatic if written by a Hollywood screen writer. Following is what happened:

That afternoon members of K Company, the "bad boy" company, were given exercise by walking in the prison yard. Their guard began marching them back to their cells in White City around 3:00 p.m. As they passed the entrance to the administrative offices, they noticed that both gates of the "bullpen" were open. The bullpen separated the prison yard from the guardroom and adjoining administrative offices. There were gates on both sides of the bullpen. The prison rule was that one of those gates had to be locked at all times. George Bennett, the captain of the guards, was leading a group of about 25 individuals who had come to visit prisoners, back into the administrative offices and neglected to keep one gate locked. (Bennett was later suspended indefinitely for his negligence.)

The Rebellion Following the Fire

When the prisoners noticed that both gates to the bullpen were open, 13 of the most dangerous criminals in the penitentiary rushed through it and into the guardroom, where they grabbed clubs hanging on the wall. They also took three pistols from a desk in the guardroom. They were already armed with self-made knives concealed in their clothing. They overpowered the guard in charge of the third, and final, steel gate between the prison yard and the administrative offices and opened that gate. They shot, stabbed, and clubbed their way through the bullpen, the guardroom, and the administrative offices to the door leading to Spring Street, which they smashed in order to gain their freedom. The escapees injured three guards, the warden's secretary, and a trusty as they made their way to freedom by stabbing and clubbing them. Seven of the convicts were shot as they made their escape, but they all made it outside. None of the injuries to the guards or prisoners were fatal, but one guard was seriously injured and hospitalized in critical condition.

Warden Thomas and Tacks Latimer were in an office upstairs. They knew from the commotion exactly what had happened. The warden handed Latimer a .45 caliber handgun and said, "Go to it." The warden then grabbed the automatic shotgun he kept in his office and went to his porch overlooking Spring Street. He waited there for the convicts to appear, and when they did, he started shooting, but didn't stop any of them. Tacks positioned himself outside the room of the warden's daughter, Amanda, (then 30 years old) to protect her. He fired at the convicts from there. Amanda was in her room getting dressed to go to a party. She also heard the commotion and figured out what was happening. She dressed as quickly as she could, grabbed a pistol, and headed downstairs. By the time she made it downstairs, the convicts had escaped. There were bullet holes in the walls, doors, and the ceiling. There was broken glass and blood on the floor. She helped where she could. She calmly called the radio stations and asked them to make the public aware of what was happening. She called the Adjutant General and requested guns and soldiers. Knowing that most of the escapees had headed toward the Toledo and Ohio Central Railroad Station, she called the train station to find out if the train that was due to depart for Toledo stopped in Marysville. She wanted to alert the sheriff's office there, if it did.

The penitentiary's administrative offices, showing the door from which the escapees exited the prison and the porch from which Warden Thomas shot at the escapees
Courtesy of the Ohio History Connection

(An Ohio Bell Telephone operator quickly notified all cities within 50 miles about the break and the pursuit of the escapees.)

One of the escapees collapsed about ten feet outside the door. He had been shot while going through the administrative offices by the warden's secretary, a former Army lieutenant. The wounded convict was immediately taken to the prison hospital.

The other prisoners kept going. One went west on Spring Street and was captured a couple of blocks from the prison by two guards who marched him back to the penitentiary.

A third convict made it to the Scioto River, which he followed north to the vicinity of the Gloria Nightclub, located on the northwest corner of Cambridge Boulevard and Dublin Road. He was spotted around 9:30 p.m. that evening by two men who told the owner of the Gloria, Sam Delewese. Delewese grabbed a gun he kept at the nightclub, and he and the two men got into Delewese's car and drove to where the convict was hiding nearby behind a pile of bricks. They captured him, and Delewese and the men drove him back to the penitentiary.

Prison guards and Tacks Latimer commandeered a car and chased the other escapees. Private citizens also joined the pursuit.

Warden Thomas joined the chase in his own car, driven by a former Cincinnati policeman serving a sentence at the penitentiary for murder. However, the warden's car broke down shortly after the chase began.

Nine of the escapees made their way to the corner of West Broad and Starling Streets where they commandeered a car. They dragged the woman out who was driving it, and all nine convicts piled in. They sped west on Broad Street at 60 mph, pursued by three police officers, Corporal Harry Kimmel, Officer George Tiller and Officer C. H. Hulls, who were on motorcycles.

During the pursuit there was a lot of gunfire back and forth between the convicts and the motorcycle policemen. A six-year-old girl was struck by a stray bullet as she was trying to cross Broad Street, but she was not seriously hurt. Officer Hulls rode his motorcycle without holding his handlebars while riding up the hill past the insane asylum on West Broad Street in order to reload his gun. Officer Tiller's motorcycle quit working at Hague Ave. The officer got into a car being driven by a civilian pursuer and continued the chase. A couple of miles from New Rome Hull's motorcycle started to die and about a half-mile from New Rome, Kimmel's motorcycle overheated and seized up. Hulls motorcycle came to a stop where Kimmel was stopped, and the two officers flagged down the car directly behind them that was also in the chase. They and the driver of that car continued the pursuit. The chase continued on Broad Street to New Rome where the convicts turned onto a road leading to Galloway, Georgesville, Lily Chapel, and London. Kimmel and Hulls, passengers in the civilian's car, followed. It was a wild ride, the car sometimes going around corners and curves on two wheels, grazing fence posts and sideswiping parked cars as it sped along.

As they were approaching Galloway, the car overheated and stopped. The policemen bailed out and got into the car behind it. It was a new Buick, and Officer Tiller, whose motorcycle had stopped running at Hague Ave., was a passenger in that car. The driver and the three policemen continued their pursuit and had nearly caught up with the convicts as they were approaching Georgesville.

They lost ground at Georgesville because the convicts made it

The Rebellion Following the Fire

across a railroad crossing, but the pursuers were held up by a passing freight train. The officers told the railroad station agent what was happening, and he called the Madison County Sheriff's office. The sheriff and some deputized men from Madison County got in the sheriff's cruiser and went east from London on the same road. They set up a roadblock near Lily Chapel, about 20 miles southwest of the penitentiary, by parking the cruiser crosswise in the middle of the road.

After the freight train had passed, the three officers and their civilian driver pursued the "bad boys" once again. They had almost caught up with them again and were exchanging gunfire when the convicts wrecked their get-away car in the ditch as they tried to get around the sheriff's roadblock.

The convicts scattered in a nearby cornfield. One of the convicts hid in a corn shock and continued shooting at the police until he ran out of ammunition. The Columbus police officers and the sheriff and his deputies captured all nine convicts, with some help by the driver of the Buick and other pursuers. The convicts were returned to the penitentiary and put in solitary confinement after being treated at the prison hospital for their wounds.

Amazingly, no one died as a result of all this drama.

Cleveland officials and residents were very upset about the prison break. Three of the escapees were considered the most notorious gunmen in the history of Cleveland. All three were serving life sentences for murder. One, Jiggs Losteiner, was the leader of a band of bank robbers. Another was a holdup man who had murdered a cashier in cold blood at a restaurant he was robbing.

The Rebellion Following the Fire

The third had murdered a patrolman and had promised that one day he would return to Cleveland and settle up old scores. At his trial, he threatened the prosecutor and attempted to throw an inkwell at the judge who sentenced him to life in prison.

There were five convicted murderers in all, among the 13 escapees.

Oliver Glaspy, the 13th escapee, was still at large at the end of the day. He was on the loose for three days. His being on the loose was a concern for everyone in Columbus because, although he wasn't a convicted murderer, he had been diagnosed as being "dangerously insane."

However, Glaspy turned out not to be a problem. On Wednesday, November 11, he went to the backdoor of a home in Groveport and begged for a sandwich. The homeowner suspected he might be the escaped prisoner who was still at large. He fed him, but then notified the Groveport mayor. The mayor, the home owner, and a marshal armed themselves and searched for Glasby. They found him behind the Hocking Valley Railroad Station. They questioned him and then took him to the village jail. He offered no resistance. The mayor called Warden Thomas. The warden sent Deputy Warden Woodard to Groveport, and he identified Glasby and took him back to the penitentiary. Glaspy, who was mentally deficient, said that when the other convicts ran toward the bullpen, he just ran along with them, not understanding what was going on. The next thing he knew, he was outside. The others told him to "scram," and he did. He didn't see the others after that.

The Continuing Investigation by The State Fire Marshal

The Continuing Investigation by The State Fire Marshal

Shortly after the fire, Warden Thomas and Deputy State Fire Marshal Joseph Clear, the investigator appointed by State Fire Marshal, Raymond Gill, to lead the investigation of the fire on his behalf, became convinced that the fire had been set by convicts, and they undertook to prove who did it and how it was done. It took them about four months of finding and talking to prisoners who were willing to tell them what they knew about the fire and in turn, talking to the convicts whose names came up in those conversations to get their first big break in solving the mystery.

Their investigation led them to James Raymond, alias Paul Sullivan. Raymond was 30 years old at the time of the fire and had been incarcerated at the penitentiary since 1923, serving a 10 to 15-year sentence for burglary and larceny.

On August 19, 1930, almost four months after the fire, Warden Thomas and Deputy Fire Marshal Clear's belief that the fire was set by inmates was confirmed when Raymond sent word to the warden that he wanted to talk and then made an oral confession to him of being involved in a plot to start a fire at the penitentiary for the purpose of facilitating an escape. He pointed his finger at two other prisoners, Hugh Gibbons and Clinton Grate, for actually starting the April 21 blaze. He said that he had supplied Grate and Gibbons with candles used in earlier attempts to start a fire, but that Jimmy Maloney furnished the candles they used in setting the fatal fire. Raymond told the warden that he feared for his life at the hands of other prisoners because of giving this information. The warden immediately put him in solitary confinement to protect him.

[NOTE: Gibbons' last name was actually Gibson, but he was

incarcerated under the name of Gibbons and was known by that name in prison. I will be referring to him as "Gibbons" herein.]

Warden Thomas and Deputy State Fire Marshal Joseph Clear were elated to have finally gotten the break in solving the mystery of the origin of the fire they had been hoping for. Now, with Raymond's help, they were confident they could get others to talk and testify in a prosecution of the guilty parties.

However, their confidence that they were about to be able to make a case against those responsible was shattered two days later, on August 21, when they learned that Raymond had committed suicide around 6:00 o'clock that morning by hanging himself from the top bar of his cell using a rope he made from his blanket. To accomplish his hanging, he stepped from a stack of blankets that had been left in the cell.

The warden and Clear responded to the setback by immediately devising a plan that they hoped would bring about confessions from Grate and Gibbons. The day after Raymond's suicide, Grate and Gibbons were put in solitary confinement. The warden had Gibbons put in the cell where Raymond had committed suicide. The rope Raymond had fashioned and hanged himself with was left tied to an overhead bar. His shoes and the blankets he had stepped from were placed beneath the rope. Grate was put in the cell directly above Gibbons, so the two suspects could talk to one another. The warden figured Grate would encourage Gibbons to kill himself, since "dead men don't tell tales." He had a trusty stationed close by Gibbons to cut him down before he died if he did attempt it.

The Continuing Investigation by The State Fire Marshal

The next morning the warden called Clear and told him the plan had worked. Grate did goad Gibbons into attempting to hang himself. Gibbons attempted it three times during the night, but didn't succeed. For one of his attempts, he used his shirt for the noose and rope, but when he stepped off the blankets, the shirt couldn't bear his weight and tore apart. He would have succeeded on his third try if the trusty hadn't cut him down.

Gibbons in solitary confinement
Courtesy of the Ohio History Connection

The warden and Clear had Grate and Gibbons brought to them. After commenting on the red welt on Gibbons' neck, the warden tried to get him to talk, but the only thing he was willing to talk about was his attempt to hang himself. He and Grate both denied that they were involved in setting the fire. When asked who had started it, they gave the name of a convict who had died in the fire.

When they refused to admit their involvement, the warden ordered that Gibbons and Grate be kept apart and prevented from talking to one another.

Warden Thomas and Joe Clear continued to interrogate prisoners hoping to obtain information they could use in the prosecution of the suspects. The next break in the case came in early March, 1931, several months after Gibbons attempted suicide.

Jimmy Maloney, a 26-year-old inmate, serving a sentence for robbery sent word to the Deputy Warden Woodard that he wanted to talk with the warden about the fire. Maloney told the warden that he had given two candles to Grate and Gibbons (taken by Maloney from the Catholic chapel), which they said they needed for some soldering they wanted to do. Maloney further said that during the fire, both Grate and Gibbons told him to keep quiet about giving them the candles because, if he didn't he would be implicated in the fire as they had used them to start the blaze. Maloney said that because he knew who had started the fire, he feared for his life. He said Grate had made a couple of attempts to kill him and asked to be put in solitary confinement. The warden complied with his request and later transferred him to a different prison facility, the Junction City brick plant, to keep him out of the reach of Grate and Gibbons.

Donald Hoskins, Franklin County Prosecutor
Courtesy of the Columbus Dispatch

The warden and Clear conferred with Franklin County Prosecutor, Donald Hoskins, but the prosecutor didn't feel that they had enough evidence to win a conviction. The information gotten from Raymond was "hearsay" and would not be admissible in court, and the testimony of Maloney would undoubtedly be refuted by Grate and Gibbons and would be characterized as one convict's word against another's. "Juries are disposed to place little faith in the word of a convict," the prosecutor said. Lawyers for Grate and Gibbons would strenuously argue that the jury should not find them guilty only on the testimony of a felon.

It was then decided to have the Franklin County grand jury conduct an investigation into the cause of the fire to see what evidence that might produce, and on Wednesday, March 25, 1931, the grand-jury began hearing testimony concerning the origin of the fire. For the remainder of the week Deputy Ohio Fire Marshal, Joseph Clear, Warden Thomas, several guards and various convicts appeared before the grand jury and gave testimony.

Prisoners who testified were naturally concerned about their safety. Steps were taken to prevent other prisoners from learning that they had testified. In order to keep the prisoner population from knowing who was testifying, no subpoenas were issued and the prisoners were brought before the grand jury individually and taken from the grand jury room before the next witness was brought in. During the process, the convicts never saw one-another. No record was kept of who testified, and the testimony of those who did testify was kept secret.

During that first week the grand jury only heard wild "cock & bull" stories and inconsequential testimony from the prisoners, and by the end of the week was on the verge of ending their investigation into the cause of the fire.

Clinton Grate and Hugh Gibbons were among the convicts who had been questioned, and both had been told that they would be recalled for further questioning during the following week.

The Confession

On Saturday, March 28, a note from Grate to Gibbons was intercepted by prison officials. The note said, "Keep your mouth shut, or else. But, if you have decided to talk, I want to know it. When you get back to the mess hall, nod your head if you are going to talk. If you are going to keep still, shake your head when I look at you. But, whatever you do, let's stick together."

The "kite" (prison language for a note) was delivered to Gibbons by Frank Mills, a prison "kite runner." Mills noticed that after reading the note, Gibbons put it in his jacket pocket and went to the mess hall for dinner. Mills followed him. Gibbons hung his jacket up on a peg before going into the dining area. Mills took the note from the jacket and carried it to the deputy warden's office where a typewritten copy was made. Mills then returned the note to the mess hall and put it back into Gibbon's jacket pocket.

The copy of the note was taken to the warden who shared its contents with Clear and then gave the note to Donald Hoskins, the prosecutor. On Monday, March 30, Grate was taken before the grand jury to testify and was questioned by Assistant Prosecutor Eugene Carlin. At first, Grate denied having anything to do with the fire. Then Carlin sprung the note on him. Grate said he would not talk about the note with anyone except Prosecutor Hoskins.

Hoskins was attending a funeral at the time. When he returned from the funeral later in the day, Grate and Gibbons were taken to Hoskins' office where he questioned them, and they both confessed. Their confessions were made in the presence of Prosecutor Hoskins, Assistant Prosecutors Eugene Carlin, Clayton Rose, and Henry Holden, Franklin County Investigator Vincent Martin, Columbus Chief of Detectives Shellenbarger, and Columbus City Detectives Otto Phillips and Otto Kaffits.

Grate and Gibbons admitted they started the fire and explained how they did it. Grate filled a pan from the mess hall used for serving potatoes with a mixture of straw oil (used by the construction crew to coat the wooden forms so concrete wouldn't stick to them) and kerosene. Grate had carried four or five gallons of the mixture in buckets to an uncompleted cell near where they started the fire and hidden it. He drove two nails through a short piece of two-by-four and affixed candles to the nails. He set the board in the pan and used two small cement blocks, approximately 2" by 2" by 3", to hold it down, setting a block on each end of the board. Then he filled the pan with enough oil that the candle was partially submerged but the top of the candle, including the wick was above the oil level.

Oil soaked wood shavings were floated in the pan. The pan was set under a pile of the wooden forms used to shape concrete. The forms had been coated with straw oil. For kindling, Grate split up two-by-fours and doused the pieces with the straw oil and kerosene mixture. He stood the pieces up around the pan where they would ignite once the candle burned down and the oil and shavings caught fire. The plan was that the wooden forms would be ignited by the kindling and, in turn, they would catch the roof on fire. The roof was less than ten feet from the top of the forms. Gibbons kept watch for guards while Grate set up the "fuse."

Grate confessed that he devised the method of starting the fire and set it up, and Gibbons confessed that he lit the fuse (the candles). They said that they had been planning the fire for almost a year and admitted that they had made three previous attempts to set the penitentiary afire; the previous attempts failed for various reasons. Candles taken from the Catholic chapel were used in all four attempts. James Raymond furnished the candles used in the three failed attempts, and Jimmy Maloney furnished the candles for the successful attempt. The first attempt was made in December when the oil soaked forms were stacked up against the prison chapel. A heavy snow that day prevented the fire from starting.

The second attempt was done when the crew constructing I&K Cellblock, was working on the third tier. (Both Grate and Gibbons were part of the crew.) The third attempt was made on Friday, April 17, (Good Friday) when they were working on the fourth tier. The second and third attempts failed because the candles went out without catching the kindling on fire.

Grate lit the candles for the three failed attempts. On Easter Monday Gibbons lit them, "to change their luck." He told Grate, "Let me light them, maybe it will be a better success this time." The candles were lit at 4:00 p.m. when the whistle blew signaling the end of the workday for the prisoners. Gibbons remarked to

The Continuing Investigation by The State Fire Marshal

Grate that if the fuse worked this time, there was a better chance of setting the roof on fire since they had set it on the fifth range, closer to the roof. Grate and Gibbons went to dinner as soon as Gibbons lit the candles. The plan was that the fire would begin while the convicts were eating their evening meal in the mess hall. When they were finished with dinner and were back in their cells and there was no sign of fire, they assumed that they had failed again, but suddenly there was a cry of "FIRE!" The conflagration had begun. Their estimate of how long it would take for the fuse to start the fire was tragically off.

Had the fire started when the prisoners were out of their cells for the evening meal, they could have rushed the gates or seized the firemen's ladders and used them to go over the wall, when the fire trucks arrived.

At the meeting with Hoskins and the others, Grate also admitted that he had urged Gibbons to commit suicide while they were in solitary confinement after Raymond's death. They said that they had made a suicide pact. Gibbons thought Grate was going to kill himself that night. Before Gibbons made his third attempt, he called up to Grate and didn't get a response. He assumed Grate had already killed himself. However, Grate hadn't even tried.

Gibbons was 34 when he started the fire. He was from Philadelphia and had been convicted of holding up a fur store in Cleveland and sentenced to 10 to 15 years in the penitentiary. He had served nine years of his sentence and would have been eligible for parole in 1931. His prison nickname was "The Jew," although he wasn't Jewish.

When the fire occurred, Grate was 30. He was from Virginia and had been convicted of holding up a gas station in Dayton and sentenced to 20-25 years in the penitentiary. He had served nine years of his sentence. His prison nickname was "Cotton."

When the fact that Grate and Gibbons had confessed as a result of an intercepted kite carried by Frank Mills, Mills was removed from the prison and taken to another prison facility for his safety.

The Trial

The Trial

Gibbons and Grate were moved from the penitentiary to the county jail on Wednesday evening in anticipation that they would be indicted. The penitentiary officials wanted them out of the prison before the news broke that they were responsible for the fire.

Convicts involved in setting the penitentiary on fire
Courtesy of the Ohio History Connection

Prior to the confessions, the grand jury was on the verge of ending their investigation into the cause of the fire, but with the confessions having been made, the grand jury returned first-degree murder indictments against Grate and Gibbons on Thursday, April 2. Specifically, they were charged: with "causing the death of a person while in the perpetration of arson of a dwelling house," which is classified as first-degree murder by the arson statutes; and were also charged with "deliberate and premeditated murder." On Friday, April 3, at a conference in the Franklin County Jail, Grate and Gibbons told Prosecuting Attorney Hoskins and reporters that they would plead guilty to first-degree murder if the court would sentence them to die immediately in the electric chair. They said they wanted to get it over with, and that they were "ready to take their medicine." "We don't want to go back to the penitentiary," said Gibbons. They asked Hoskins whether they would be executed if they pled guilty. Hoskins replied that it would be up to the judge.

Then, they asked if they could talk with the judge before their arraignment. Hoskins told them that on Monday, before the arraignment, attorneys would be appointed to represent them, and they could discuss the matter with them.

Gibbons again admitted lighting the fuse that started the fire, but said, "I didn't know it would take so many lives. We only wanted to burn down the cellblock, because we didn't want other prisoners to live in it. The thing has been on my mind ever since the fire. I have gone through hell." He also talked about his attempts to end his life while in solitary confinement. "I'll not

Prosecutor Donald Hoskins on right, talked to Clinton Grate and Hugh Gibbons (hand on face), as jailor Henry Beard looked on. The prisoners told Hoskins they didn't want to go back to the penitentiary and asked if they could be immediately put to death in the electric chair if they pled guilty.

try it again. I'm going to take my medicine," said Gibbons. They both denied that they set the fire to facilitate an escape. Gibbons said, "We didn't plan to escape. I was in my cell when the fire came in, and a guard let me out. I helped carry other prisoners out, and I also had to carry a guard down part of the range when the smoke got him."

On Saturday, April 4, Judge Cecil Randall, who would preside at their arraignment and trial, declined to meet with Grate and Gibbons. The arraignment was set for Monday, April 6, 1931, which happened to be the day after Easter that year. The fire occurred on the day after Easter the year before. On Monday, April 6, before the arraignment, attorneys John Connor and Dwight Swisher were named to defend Gibbons, and William Bartels and John Eagleson were named to defend Grate. After a short conference with their attorneys, Grate and Gibbons were arraigned before Judge Randall and pled not guilty to the charges.

The defense attorneys told their clients, and after the arraignment told reporters, that they believed the indictment was defective, and that they would attack it. It was their contention that the prosecution could not produce any evidence that the defendants intended for anyone to be harmed as a result of their actions, and therefore, it was not "deliberate and premeditated murder." They also contended that the statute which provided that causing the death of a person "while in the perpetration of arson" constitutes first-degree murder did not apply, because the legislature had amended the statute in 1929 and limited its application to arson of a "dwelling house" and that the penitentiary is not a "dwelling house."

The Trial

They also stated that they could prove that the electrical wiring at the penitentiary was defective, and the defective wiring or spontaneous combustion could have been the cause of the blaze that killed the prisoners. They contended that although Grate and Gibbons had confessed to trying to start a "bon-fire," that fire might not have been responsible for the deaths, and the prosecution had the burden of proving that the fire that killed the prisoners was not caused by the defective wiring or spontaneous combustion of long accumulated dust and dirt in out of the way places in the prison. Bartels said to reporters, "These men say that they tried to start a fire, but they went away immediately after it was kindled, and whether their attempt was successful is not known, in our opinion." "I'll miss my guess if these men are ever sent to the electric chair," Bartels confidently said.

That morning, before the arraignment proceedings had begun, both Grate and Gibbons made statements to the reporters who were present, which implied that Jimmy Maloney was lying when he said he didn't know they planned to use the candles to set the penitentiary on fire, and Grate denied he had attempted to "bump off" Maloney.

Maloney who had agreed to testify against Grate and Gibbons, told authorities that he had received threats from "co-conspirators" at the brick plant where he was now being housed, and because of that, Prosecutor Hoskins had him transferred to the Franklin County jail.

Grate's trial began on Monday, May 18. Grate was dressed in a dark-blue suit, green tie, white shirt, and dark shoes, all of which had been furnished by his relatives. Gibbons' trial was scheduled

The Trial

to begin after the conclusion of Grate's trial.

Thirty-three-year-old Donald Hoskins graduated from The Ohio State University Law School in 1924 and had only recently become the Franklin County Prosecutor. He was elected in November 1930, defeating the incumbent, John J. (Jack) Chester. This was his first prosecution of a murder case. Likewise, Judge Randall was new to his position, having been elected at the November 1930 election to his first term as a common pleas judge, and this was his first murder case.

In early May, the defense attorneys announced that, if the court approved, John Connor and Dwight Swisher, the attorneys representing Gibbons, would team up with Grate's attorneys, William Bartels and John Eagleson, and the four of them would represent Grate. Therefore, the first matter to be determined at Grate's trial was whether the judge would allow Connor

At the first day of Grate's trial, John Connors (standing) argues that he and Dwight Swisher should be allowed to be part of Grate's defense team
Courtesy of the Ohio History Center

and Swisher to become part of Grate's defense team. Over the objection of Prosecutor Hoskins, Judge Randall ruled that they could. The rest of the first day was spent selecting members of

The Trial

the jury. Seven were tentatively selected by the end of the day. The defense added nine names to the list of convicts that they would call as witnesses, bringing the total to 29. Hoskins stated that he intended to call nine convicts as witnesses for the prosecution.

On Tuesday, May 19, Ohio Penitentiary Warden Thomas moved the prisoners who were to testify at the trial to the county jail. Hoskins immediately had prisoners whom he intended to call as witnesses, including Jimmy Maloney, segregated from the defense witnesses by moving them from the county jail to the city jail.

Jury selection was completed on the morning of the third day, Wednesday, May 20.

In the early afternoon, opening statements were made by Prosecutor Hoskins for the State of Ohio and by John Connor for the defense. In his opening statement, Prosecutor Hoskins declared that Grate and Gibbons had started the fire intending to escape, and to enable their friends to escape during the chaos that would follow. He then explained how they had started the fire.

Appearing on behalf of Grate, Attorney Connor declared that the fire was caused by defective wiring and that if any lives were lost it was due to incompetent administration, lack of leadership, and negligence. He declared that Captain Hall was negligent when, in response to being informed that there was smoke in the top cells, he ordered Guard Watkinson not to let the prisoners out, but just to open the windows to give them some air, then walked away, and never returned to change the order.

The Trial

It was announced that Joseph Clear, the deputy state fire marshal, who investigated the prison blaze and was one of the principal witnesses for the state had been stricken with a severe attack of appendicitis Tuesday evening. His physician advised him to go to the hospital, but he refused because of the trial and stayed in bed at his home. The physician planned to examine him again on Thursday. The possibility was discussed that the jury, the defendant, the lawyers, the judge, and other court personnel might be taken to his home or the hospital and court held there to take his testimony.

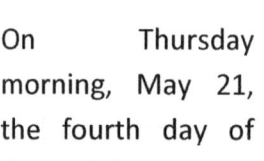

Wooden models of "G&H," "I&K," and "L" Cellblocks prepared as exibiits for the trial, shown with Prosecutor Donald Hoskins at left and Assistant Prosecutor Clayton Rose beside him – Clinton Grate pictured at bottom left

On Thursday morning, May 21, the fourth day of the trial, it was announced that Joe Clear had gone to the hospital and had an appendectomy.

On that morning, in an attempt to bolster the claim that the arson was in a dwelling house, the prosecutor introduced evidence that the residence of the warden, his wife, and his daughter shared a

The Trial

roof with the cell block where the prisoners died and that the roof was part of the same building.

The defense, in cross-examining prosecution witnesses, attempted to establish that there were wiring problems within the building that might have been the real cause of the fire that killed the prisoners rather than the acts of Grate and Gibbons.

After lunch, the jury was taken to the penitentiary to view the scene of the fire.

Later in the afternoon, 26-year-old Ohio Penitentiary inmate, Jimmy Maloney, was called to the witness stand by Hoskins. He testified:

That Grate and Gibbons told him they set the fire at the penitentiary that resulted in the death of 320 convicts.

That he lived in fear for his life after the fire because of his knowledge of who had set it.

That prior to the fire, at their request, he furnished Grate and Gibbons with two candles, about two or three inches long, which were taken from the Catholic chapel inside the prison.

That they told him they needed the candles to do some soldering work.

That at quitting time on the day of the fire, he saw Grate and Gibbons come out of a door next to the I&K Cellblock, and that they acted nervous and kept looking around.

That he saw Grate when the fire was raging. Grate said to him,

"Jimmy, this is awful. Don't tell anybody you give me those candles." He asked why, and Grate said," If you do, you'll be implicated. Those candles were used to set the fire."

That Gibbons came up to him a little later and, in substance, said that he and Grate had set the place on fire and to set it, had used the two candles he had given them.

That they both told him how they had rigged the candles up on a two-by-four and put it in a potato pan filled with oil.

That Grate was his "shadow after the fire because everywhere I went, he was behind me.... Grate's idea was to get me in a secluded spot, and that would be the last of me."

That two days after the fire, he saw Grate in the blacksmith shop grinding a file. Grate invited him in to help turn the wheel. Maloney declined.

That on the Saturday following the fire, Grate lunged at him with a knife. He reported the attack to Captain Laukart and for his safety, Maloney was put in solitary confinement.

That in the anteroom, while he was waiting to be called as a witness, Grate told him, "Jimmy, don't say anything. Stand pat." He further said that the conversation was heard by Deputy Sheriff Ephraim Gordon.

On cross-examination, he was asked if he had anything against Grate and responded, "I always liked 'Cotton.' I have nothing against Grate whatever."

On redirect he said that Grate and Gibbons had told him their

The Trial

reason for starting the fire was to "start a commotion and get the pig (Warden Thomas)."

On the fifth day of the trial, Friday, May 22, Roy Taylor testified that he had recently been Grate's cellmate (earlier in 1931) and while they were cellmates, Grate told him he set the "fuse" that started the fire and Gibbons lit it. He also testified to other admissions made by Grate that verified testimony previously given by Jimmy Maloney.

Deputy Sheriff Gordon took the stand and, concerning Maloney's testimony that Grate told Maloney in the anteroom not to say anything, he testified that he heard Grate say the words "say nothing," but that was all he heard.

Convict David Monypeny, who occupied the cell beside Grate's at the time of the fire, testified that around 2:30 p.m. on the day of the fire he saw Grate carrying an oil can in the area where the fire began. He also testified that, after supper Grate told him, "Get ready to leave tonight." When he asked why, Grate told him, "You'll find out later."

On Monday, May 25, the sixth day of the trial, Judge Randall ruled that the confession made by Grate to Prosecutor Hoskins, the assistant prosecutors, and the detectives on March 30, was admissible. It was read to the jury.

Sheriff Harry Paul and one of his deputies, Charles Hoff, then told the jury that after the confessions were made, Grate took them to the spot where the fuse was set.

Next, inmate Frank Mills testified that he was a prison "kite

The Trial

runner" and that he carried a "kite" from Grate to Gibbons on Saturday, March 28, two days before Grate confessed. When delivered, Gibbons read the note, put it in his jacket pocket and then went to the mess hall. Mills followed Gibbons to the mess hall. Gibbons hung his jacket up on a peg before going into the dining hall. Mills took the note from the pocket, and took it to the deputy warden's office, where a typewritten copy was made. Mills then put it back in Gibbon's pocket.

The typewritten copy of the note was identified by Mills as a copy of the note that he delivered to Gibbons and then took to the deputy warden's office. It was introduced into evidence.

Mills was followed on the witness stand by the prisoner who copied the note in the deputy warden's office.

This was the note set forth above that resulted in the confessions by Grate and Gibbons.

On the morning of the seventh day of the trial, Tuesday, May 26, before the trial resumed, County Prosecutor Hoskins, along with his assistants and the defense attorneys, met with Judge Randall in the judge's chambers. After a conference lasting about a half hour, the trial resumed and additional evidence was presented by the prosecutor.

Two newspaper reporters, Samuel Fusco and Ralph Henney each testified that they interviewed Grate and Gibbons at the county jail, and they admitted setting the fire. The defendants also insisted to the reporters that Jimmy Maloney was in on the plot. They said that Maloney knew what the candles were for that he

The Trial

had obtained for them from the Catholic chapel.

Then two reporters testified that Grate had admitted to them his part in setting the fire and said he would rather be electrocuted than returned to the penitentiary.

The confession of Grate and Gibbons was then read to the jury.

The final two witnesses were Sheriff Harry Paul and one of his deputies, Charles Huff. Sheriff Paul told the jury that Grate and Gibbons each had separately taken him to the spot where the fire was started. Deputy Huff's testimony was identical to the sheriff's.

Thereupon, Prosecutor Hoskins rested his case against Clinton Grate.

It was expected that defense counsel, at that point, would move to dismiss the first-degree murder charges, arguing that no evidence had been introduced to show Grate had meant to kill inmates, and that the penitentiary was not a "dwelling house."

Instead, defense counsel, the prosecutor, and the assistant prosecutors returned to chambers to confer again with the judge. After a short time, the conference was moved to the consultation room, where it continued until noon. Then they returned to the courtroom, and the judge adjourned the trial until 1:30 in the afternoon.

When court reconvened at 1:30 p.m., defendant Grate pled guilty to second-degree murder, and upon being asked by the judge, he assured the court that his guilty plea was made of his own free will. Prosecutor Hoskins agreed to drop his contention that Grate had deliberately killed the prisoners and agreed not to pursue the charge that Grate committed first-degree murder by causing the death of a person "while in the perpetration of arson in a dwelling house." Judge Randall accepted Grate's guilty plea to second-degree murder and sentenced him to life in prison at the penitentiary. The sentence would begin after he had finished serving his sentence for his robbery conviction. That ended Grate's trial.

Hugh Gibbons was then brought before the court, and he also changed his plea to guilty of second-degree murder. He received the same sentence as Grate.

After finding the defendants guilty of second-degree murder and sentencing them to life in prison, Judge Randall said to the jury and the other people in the courtroom, "It might not be inappropriate at this time to make observations of some phases of this case. The law is somewhat in doubt as to the arson statute." He continued by explaining that the 1929 amendments to the arson statutes made the first-degree murder provision applicable only to arson of dwelling houses and left doubt as to what types of buildings were intended to be classified as dwelling houses under the statute and whether the Ohio Penitentiary was intended to be so classified. He then said that he was calling this "to the attention of the public at this time for the reason that the legislature is now in session."

Prosecutor Hoskins then explained his position in accepting the plea. He said: "The prosecutor's office accepted this plea of guilty to murder in the second degree because we found no direct evidence of intent to kill on behalf of either defendant.... There is no direct positive evidence to establish that the burning of any human being was within the contemplation of either of the defendants...."

"This office was also induced to accept the plea of murder in the second degree by reason of the status of Ohio Penitentiary under sections of the general code having to do with arson. The Legislature, in its 1929 codification, has left considerable doubt as to whether the penitentiary is a dwelling house. We believe that life imprisonment is a just sentence on behalf of the defendants and on behalf of the State of Ohio."

On Tuesday, shortly after they were sentenced by Judge Randall, Grate and Gibbons were returned to the Ohio Penitentiary where they were put in solitary confinement near the north end of I&K Cellblock, a short distance from the place where they started the fire.

Grate (left) and Gibbons (right), with heads bowed, return to the penitentiary after their convictions
Courtesy of the Columbus Dispatch

Epilogue

Epilogue

Living under the gazes of men who had experienced the fire and could have died, and unable to live with the thought of what he had done to his fellow inmates any longer, Clinton Grate hanged himself in his cell at dawn on January 15, 1933, with a noose made of a braided sheet from his bed. He was found by a guard hanging from the ceiling of his cell at 7:00 o'clock in the morning.

At the time of his death, Grate was housed in White City, in a cell by himself. From his cell he could see the prison yard and a memorial to the victims of the fire, built by the prisoners. Prisoners said that he was always very quiet and melancholy. Penitentiary officials said that he continually brooded and at times appeared insane.

After he had hanged himself, guards found a copy of that week's edition of the *Columbus Sunday Star*, a weekly publication, under his bed. It was opened to an article about the fire.

It was reported by Warden Thomas that after going back to prison, Gibbons made further attempts to kill himself, but always failed. He died at the penitentiary on July 23, 1973, a broken and haunted old man.

Who else was involved in the plot to set fire to the penitentiary was never established. There were reports that the investigators believed there were a total of seven conspirators, two of whom had died in the fire. No evidence was presented implicating James Raymond in the fire that killed the convicts, although he was involved in the three failed attempts to start a fire, by supplying candles to Grate and Gibbons.

Epilogue

Although Grate and Gibbons denied that their purpose in setting the fire was to facilitate an escape, it was widely believed that it was their real motive, and because it went so tragically wrong, they quickly abandoned the idea.

Blame

Some blame for the great loss of life was directed by the public at prison officials and guards for decisions they made while dealing with the fire, but the blame was mitigated by an understanding that a fire of that magnitude was not within their contemplation in a cellblock such as the G&H Cellblock, and also by an understanding that they had an imperative obligation to the public to keep prisoners within the penitentiary walls.

Criticism was also directed at the governor, the state legislature, and ultimately to the citizens of Ohio for their unwillingness to furnish sufficient tax money to provide a better and a safer prison than the 96-year-old penitentiary.

In a letter to the governor of Ohio a year before the fire, the head of the Prisoners' Relief Society characterized the Ohio Penitentiary as being "an outpost of hell" and warned of troubles at the institution if conditions weren't improved. After the fire, he chastised the governor for not heeding his warning.

The National Society of Penal Information had also criticized the prison for its primitive facilities and overcrowding. As to overcrowding in Ohio's prisons, its 1929 report stated: "The ancient plant at the state penitentiary in Columbus, one of the largest prisons in the country, suffers from a condition of overcrowding worse than that in any other prison."

Of course, the ultimate responsibility and blame must be given to Clinton Grate and Hugh Gibbons.

About The Author

Donald G. Rose was born and raised in Dublin, Ohio, where he attended school from the first grade through graduation in 1956 from Dublin High School. He attended The Ohio State University and graduated with a Bachelor of Science Degree in mathematics in 1963. During the period from 1960-1962, Don served 27 months in the U.S. Army.

After his graduation from undergraduate school, he was admitted to The Ohio State University College of Law. He graduated in 1966 and later that year, after passing the bar examination, was admitted to the Ohio bar and began practicing law. From 1969 until 1971, the author was a partner in the law firm of Chester, Rose & Bolon and from 1971 until 1981, was a partner in the firm of Chester, Hoffman, Park, Willcox & Rose, which was renamed Chester, Saxbe and Willcox in 1978. He left that firm in 1981 and formed a partnership with his law school classmate, Erick Alden.

The author

Don has held various positions in the community, including the following: Dublin Village Solicitor, the attorney for the Village of Dublin, 1967-1974; member of the Mid-Ohio Regional Planning Commission, 1969-1972; and member of the State Underground Parking Commission, 1969-1985. He was chairman of the Underground Parking Commission for four years.

About The Author

In 1986, Don and his wife, Robin, a registered nurse, temporarily left their professions to go on an extended sailing adventure lasting 2 ½ years, during which they traveled 11,000 miles. After their sailing adventure, they traveled extensively in foreign countries on two trips. The first trip was for 10 ½ months in Mexico, Central America, and South America. The second trip was for 6 ½ months and took them around-the-world.

When they returned from their travels in 1992, Don resumed the practice of law as a sole practitioner. He retired in 2010.

He and Robin have continued to travel since 1992. Don's hobbies include playing duplicate bridge with his brother, Clayton Rose, his regular partner; cooking; and doing special projects such as writing books. This is his third book. His first book tells the story of cruising with his wife for 2 ½ years on their 30-foot sailboat and is entitled *Cruising Aboard The Sailboat Robin Lee*. It is based on a journal kept by Robin. His second book is entitled *Judge Clayton Rose, Sr.* and is a biography of his father.

Made in United States
North Haven, CT
21 February 2024

49002619R00095